ACCEPTANCE

AND

COMMITMENT

THERAPY WORKBOOK

THE COMPLETE ACT TOOLKIT TO STOP OVERTHINKING, CONQUER ANXIETY, OVERCOME OCD, AND FIND LASTING PEACE

VIVIAN WHITMORE

contents

BOOK 1: THE ACT PATH TO EMOTIONAL FREEDOM
A BEGINNER'S GUIDE TO ACCEPTANCE AND
COMMITMENT THERAPY FOR LASTING EMOTIONAL
RESILIENCE

Chapter 1: Understanding ACT --------------------------------- 11

Chapter 2: Acceptance as Liberation ------------------------- 18

Chapter 3: Mindfulness for Emotional Regulation ---------- 24

Chapter 4: Understanding Personal Values ------------------ 34

Chapter 5: Taking Action on Your Values -------------------- 47

Conclusion --- 63

BOOK 2: MINDFULNESS AND RADICAL ACCEPTANCE
SCIENCE-BACKED STRESS MANAGEMENT TECHNIQUES
TO FIND PEACE AND BALANCE

Introduction --- 67

Chapter 1: Understanding Stress -------------------------------- 68

Chapter 2: Mindfulness for Everyday Calm ------------------- 77

Chapter 3: Radical Acceptance in Action --------------------- 88

Chapter 4: Emotional Clarity with ACT Tools --------------- 98

Chapter 5: Sustaining Mindfulness Practices --------------- 111

Conclusion --- 124

BOOK 3: ACT FOR OVERTHINKING AND OCD
PRACTICAL TOOLS TO BREAK FREE FROM INTRUSIVE THOUGHTS AND RECLAIM MENTAL CLARITY

Introduction -- 127

Chapter 1: The Overthinking Mind --------------------------- 128

Chapter 2: Defusing Thoughts comprehensively ----------- 141

Chapter 3: Mindfulness for Mental Clarity ------------------ 157

Chapter 4: Embracing Uncertainty ---------------------------- 168

Chapter 5: Living Beyond Loops ---------------------------- 174

Conclusion -- 186

BOOK 4: BREAKING ANXIETY'S GRIP
ACT-BASED STRATEGIES TO CONQUER FEAR, FIND COURAGE, AND ALIGN WITH YOUR VALUES

Introduction -- 189

Chapter 1: Understanding Anxiety --------------------------- 190

Chapter 2: Defusing Anxious Thoughts --------------------- 204

Chapter 3: Radical Acceptance of Fear ----------------------- 213

Chapter 4: Building Your Fear Response Toolkit ------------ 220

Chapter 5: Building Courage --------------------------------- 229

Conclusion -- 242

THE ACT SELF-THERAPY TOOLKIT
A COMPLETE GUIDE TO LIFELONG EMOTIONAL GROWTH AND PSYCHOLOGICAL FLEXIBILITY

Introduction -- 245

Chapter 1: Foundations of Self-Therapy ------------------------ 246

Chapter 2: The Integration Process ------------------------------ 256

Chapter 3: Creating Your Healing Environment ------------- 267

Chapter 4: Transforming Self-Critical Patterns ------------- 277

Chapter 5: Sustaining Long-Term Growth -------------------- 289

Conclusion -- 301

Introduction

Slow down and lower the expectations you place on yourself until you feel the grip of control starting to loosen. Your mind overflows with strategies, solutions, and endless attempts to fix what feels broken inside. You force positive thoughts, challenge every anxious moment, analyze each obsession, and push yourself to confront every fear—yet the promised peace of mindfulness remains just out of reach, no matter how hard you try.

A paradox lives in this struggle because life slips through our fingers when we grip it too hard, and our brilliant minds that solve external problems with ease only tangle us further when we turn them toward our internal battles. Something deeper calls us toward a different approach that invites us to unlearn our patterns and watch what unfolds when we stop forcing change.

Although the mind protests this invitation because it wants to solve, fix, and control every aspect of our experience, breakthrough often comes through softening rather than force as healing emerges when we lay down our weapons against ourselves. Research reveals what our hearts already know—acceptance creates change that control cannot touch, while flexibility builds strength that rigidity will never match.

These pages weave together science and soul, research, and real-world practice, speaking to the part of you that knows another way exists to live with the mind you have and hold the feelings that arise as you move toward what matters, even when fear walks beside you. Through structured practices and careful exploration, you will learn to work with your mind rather than against it while discovering how to hold pain differently and keep your heart open amid uncertainty.

This book invites you to step out of the exhausting cycle of fix-and-fight toward a path that offers more than just feeling good; it guides you toward feeling whole and engaging fully with life while carrying whatever arises within you. Take these practices and exercises as your companions on this journey, using them to build a different relationship with your experiences. Start today, right where you are, with whatever you're carrying. Turn the page and begin.

Book One

THE ACT PATH
TO EMOTIONAL FREEDOM

A Beginner's Guide To Acceptance and
Commitment Therapy For Lasting
Emotional Resilience

Chapter One

UNDERSTANDING ACT

Most of us learn at an early stage that uncomfortable feelings are problems to be solved. We inherit a simple equation: Bad feelings go in one column, good feelings in another. Then we spend decades trying to maximize one column while minimizing the other. But what if this fundamental math was flawed? What if our relentless pursuit of feeling good has been quietly carrying us away from living well?

Think of how many moments you've missed while trying to calm your anxiety. How many connections you've held at arm's length while waiting to feel more confident. How many sunsets, conversations, or opportunities have slipped by while you were caught in the spiral of trying to think your way out of thinking too much?

We're taught to believe that happiness means feeling good most of the time. That anxiety should be conquered, sadness overcome and anger managed. Our culture sells us endless strategies for positive thinking, countless tools for relaxation, and infinite paths to peace. And still, something feels missing.

Look closely at the people you admire most. Notice how they move through the world. Perhaps what draws you to them isn't their perpetual happiness or their freedom from doubt. Maybe it's their capacity to embrace the full spectrum of being alive—to laugh deeply while carrying grief, to move toward what matters even as fear whispers its familiar warnings, to stay soft in a world that invites hardening.

SIMPLIFYING DEFUSION

Your mind tells you stories all day long. When anxiety hits, it warns "I can't handle this meeting." When OCD kicks in, it demands, "Check the door again or something bad will happen." Depression might whisper "Nothing will ever get better." These thoughts feel like absolute truth when they show up.

Defusion helps you create space between you and these thoughts. Instead of getting caught up in them, you learn to see them as just words your mind makes up—like clouds passing through the sky or cars driving past your house. When the thought "I'm a failure" appears, rather than letting it drag you down, you can notice, "Ah, my mind is doing that thing again where it tells me I'm failing" and continue with your day.

Think about your morning so far. How many times have you tried to argue with worried thoughts or push away the ones you don't want? It's exhausting. Defusion offers an easier way. Instead of fighting these thoughts or trying to prove them wrong, you learn to hold them lightly.

Here's what this looks like in real life: You're sitting in a meeting when your mind pipes up with "Everyone thinks I'm an idiot." Instead of believing this thought or trying to debate it, defusion helps you see it as just another story your protective mind has made up. You can notice it and still focus on what matters in that moment—contributing to the meeting, connecting with colleagues, and sharing your ideas.

Practical Defusion Techniques

An African proverb tells us: "The eye that leaves the village sees more clearly when it returns." When we step back from our village, we see home with fresh eyes. The same happens with our thoughts. Standing too close to worried thoughts, swimming in self-criticism, and drowning in OCD thoughts block us from seeing what these thoughts really are—just words our minds create.

These three techniques show you how to step back from thoughts that tangle you up. They cut through confusion and create space between you and the stories your mind tells. They work because they shift how you see thoughts, not because they try to change them.

Recording Exercise

This exercise brings this wisdom into direct practice. Open your phone's voice recorder right now and speak one of your anxious thoughts aloud—perhaps that worry about tomorrow's presentation or the doubt about a recent decision. Play it back and listen to it repeat for two full minutes. The words begin to shift, becoming just sounds rather than heavy truths. Your mind naturally starts to hear "I'm not prepared" as a collection of sounds rather than a solid fact.

Voice Change

This one works right in the moment when thoughts feel overwhelming. When your mind throws "You'll make a mistake" at you, shift it into a voice you know well. Hearing your worried thoughts in Kermit the Frog's voice or Morgan Freeman's deep tones changes how your brain processes them. The thought loses its iron grip not because you fought it, but because you transformed how you hear it.

The "I'm Having the Thought" Label

Right now, you will create instant breathing room for yourself. When your mind serves up "I'll fail," simply add "I'm having the thought that" in front. This small addition helps your brain recognize it's seeing a thought, not a fact, about reality. Use this technique anywhere —in meetings, during difficult conversations, while facing challenges.

Start first with the thoughts that carry less emotional weight before working with the ones that really hook you. The more you get familiar with these techniques, the more you'll find yourself naturally creating space around difficult thoughts instead of getting tangled in them.

AVOIDANCE: THE COST OF PLAYING IT SAFE

There's a moment I keep coming back to: A child stands at the edge of a pool, toes curled over the concrete, body tense with both desire and fear. The water beckons. Other kids splash and laugh. But for this child, the gap between wanting and doing feels enormous. Sound familiar?

Avoidance is stepping back from the things that make us anxious or uncomfortable. Like when fear rises, our minds push us to retreat because distance from discomfort brings with it quick relief. This is a pattern that we adopt early on; anxiety spikes, we decide to leave, and we feel better. OCD thoughts flood in, we check one more time, then the fear subsides. Social pressure mounts, we stay home, and the tension eases.

But this avoidance carries a hidden cost; each time we step back from a challenge, we teach our brains that retreat equals safety. This might work in the short term, but over time it creates a trap. The more we avoid, the more our brain labels situations as dangerous, and the harder it becomes to face them. What starts as skipping one social event can grow into isolation. What begins as checking something twice can expand into hours of rituals.

Our instinct to avoid pain makes sense—our brains evolved to protect us from danger. But in today's world, this protective response often holds us back from what matters most. Breaking free from avoidance starts with understanding this pattern. Only then can we learn to step forward, even when our minds signal to retreat.

SMALL STEPS, REAL CHANGE

Every summer, my friends and I go to a lake house in Maine. There's a dock that stretches out into deep water, and every year, I watch as people take running leaps off the end, plunging into the cool darkness below. For years, I stood back, telling myself I was content just watching. The water looked too deep, too cold, too uncertain. But each year, something in me longed to feel that moment of flight.

Last summer, I found myself inching closer to the edge. Not to jump-just to look. Then I sit with my feet in the water. Then climb down the ladder, holding tight to the rungs. Small steps. Tiny choices. Until one ordinary afternoon, without fanfare or ceremony, I let go of the ladder and swam out into deeper water.

Working with avoidance follows a similar path. We don't start with our biggest fears or longest-held patterns. Instead, we begin with small moves that feel possible, even if they make our hearts beat a little faster. Here's how:

❑ Start with what you can see right in front of you. Look for the tiny moments where you habitually step back from life. Maybe it's checking your phone when conversations get personal. Or taking the long way to avoid running into certain people. Or filling empty spaces with noise so you don't have to sit with uncomfortable thoughts.

❑ Choose one small avoidance to work with. Pick something manageable. Something possible to face, even if it makes your stomach flutter. If you usually text, try calling. If you always say "maybe later," say "yes" once. If you check things three times, try two.

❏ The goal here becomes simple: getting curious. What happens when you stay in that meeting five minutes longer? When you leave one email unchecked? When you let that anxious thought sit there without rushing to make it go away?

EXERCISE: IDENTIFYING YOUR AVOIDANCE PATTERNS

Take a quiet moment with paper and pen. I want you to think about an area in your life where avoidance leads you to step back instead of forward. Pick one specific situation-not your biggest fear, but one that affects your daily life.

Write down your situation:

What exactly do you avoid? Name the specific actions, places, or moments that trigger your step-back response. Instead of writing "social situations," specify "eating lunch in the break room" or "speaking up in team meetings."

Notice your escape routes:

How do you avoid this situation? Write down your exact behaviors. Do you call in sick, make excuses, check your phone, or find tasks to keep you busy? Be specific about your avoidance strategies.

Track the impact:

What does this avoidance cost you? Avoidance costs you. Not just the big costs, but the small daily ones too. Write down how stepping back affects your work, your relationships, and your sense of capability. Notice what you miss out on each time you retreat.

What can you change:

Imagine taking one small step toward what you avoid. Not diving in completely, but moving slightly closer. What tiny action could you take? What support would help you take that step?

Keep this exercise in close proximity. Add to it as you notice more patterns. Use it as a map to understand where avoidance shows up in your life and what it takes from you. This awareness creates the foundation for change.

Your mind will protest. It will list all the reasons why avoidance is safer, smarter, and better, what I encourage you to do is to thank it for trying to protect you. Then watch what happens when you take that small step anyway. Notice how the anticipation often feels worse than the moment itself. How the sky stays firmly in place when you face what you've been avoiding. How each tiny act of courage makes the next one a little more possible. In the next chapter, we'll look at how acceptance can set us free.

Chapter Two

ACCEPTANCE
AS LIBERATION

There's an old Zen story about two monks who encounter a woman unable to cross a muddy road. The first monk picks her up, carries her across, and sets her down. Hours later, the second monk, still troubled, says "We're not supposed to touch women." The first monk replies, "I set her down hours ago. Why are you still carrying her?"

This simple story captures something essential about human suffering. Like the second monk, we often carry our distress long after the actual moment has passed. That argument from this morning plays on repeat in your mind at dinner. That mistake from last week keeps you awake at night. That awkward moment from months ago still makes your cheeks burn when you remember it.

Our minds excel at this kind of carrying because they replay conversations, rehearse future scenarios, and review past mistakes with remarkable dedication. And while this mental time travel sometimes helps us learn and prepare, it more often leaves us stuck—rehashing what we can't change or worrying about what we can't control.

Think about what you're carrying right now. Maybe it's anxiety about an upcoming event, replaying every possible scenario. Or shame about something you said, examining it from every angle. Or anger about an incident that's long over but still feels fresh. Like the second monk, you might be following all the rules, doing everything "right," yet still feel burdened by what you're carrying.

This is where acceptance enters—not as resignation or defeat, but as the simple recognition that we can set down what we've been carrying. Not because we should or must, but because it's possible.

THE NATURE OF PAIN

Most of us understand physical pain. Touch a hot stove and your hand jerks back. Stub your toe—you hop around cursing. The pain is clear, direct, and serves a purpose. But emotional pain works differently. It gets complicated, tangled, layered.

Let's make this simple: There are two kinds of pain in our emotional world. The first kind—clean pain—is like that hot stove. It's the raw, natural response to life's hard moments. The grief when you lose someone you love. The fear before a major change. The anxiety before an important presentation. This pain is normal, natural, and useful—like a warning light on your car's dashboard.

Then there's dirty pain. This is the extra suffering we create by fighting the first kind of pain. It's telling yourself, "I shouldn't feel this sad" when you're grieving. It's panicking about feeling anxious. It's feeling ashamed of feeling afraid. It's like having a warning light come on in your car and then beating yourself up for being the kind of person whose car has warning lights.

Here's the difference in action:

❑ Clean pain: "I feel anxious about this presentation."

❑ Dirty pain: "I'm such a mess for feeling anxious. No one else gets this nervous. What's wrong with me?"

❑ Clean pain: "I miss my ex."

❑ Dirty pain: "It's been six months, I should be over this by now. I'm wasting my life feeling sad."

❑ Clean pain: "These OCD thoughts scare me."

❑ Dirty pain: "I'm broken for having these thoughts. I need to figure out how to never have them again."

Understanding this difference isn't just academic-it's liberation. Because while we can't always control clean pain, dirty pain is optional. We create it, and we can learn to stop creating it.

SIMPLE TOOLS FOR LETTING GO

A couple of years ago, my therapist said something that shifted everything for me. We were talking about acceptance-that loaded word that often feels like giving up. He leaned forward in his chair and said, "We tend to have a warped perception about letting go. It's not about resigning yourself and hoping for the best. It's about trusting that there will be something solid to catch you when you finally release your grip."

It reminded me of the time I went paragliding. When I was standing on the edge of that cliff, every instinct screamed to step back, to stay firmly on solid ground. The instructor kept saying, "Just keep walking forward. The wind will catch you." It felt impossible to trust that invisible force. But when I finally took those steps, the updraft caught the chute and lifted me into the air. In that moment, I understood something profound about trust. It feels terrifying until you're actually floating, supported by something you can't see but can absolutely feel.

This is what real acceptance feels like. Not a passive surrender, but an active trust in our capacity to be with whatever shows up in our lives. It's about learning to soar with our emotions rather than fighting against them.

Let's start with something simple:

The 3-Minute Pause. Not an hour of meditation. Not a weekend retreat. Just three minutes to notice what's happening inside you right now.

Here's how: Find a quiet spot. Set a timer for three minutes. Close your eyes if that feels comfortable. Now, notice three things:

☐ What's happening in your body? Maybe your shoulders are tight. Your stomach is churning. Your jaw is clenched.

☐ What emotions are moving through you? Name them simply: "Anxiety is here." "Sadness is visiting." "Frustration is present."

☐ What's on your mind? Let the thoughts come and go without trying to change them or fix them.

That's it. There is no need to feel peaceful, calm, or enlightened. No need to make anything different. Just three minutes of honest noticing.

When you're doing this, you're basically cleaning out a cluttered closet. You don't have to organize everything at once, or have to throw anything away. Just shine a light in there and see what's actually present. Your mind will try to resist this practice. It will tell you you're doing it wrong, that you should feel different, that this isn't helping. Notice these thoughts too. They're part of the process, like the tension before learning to float.

Daily Check-In Signal

Just like my paragliding instructor kept checking his instruments before each flight, this simple practice helps you read your own signals before moving through your day. It's not about fixing what you find—it's about knowing where you stand.

Here's how: Set aside a few minutes, ideally at the same time each day-maybe with your morning coffee or during your evening commute. Ask yourself three simple questions:

❑ "What's showing up right now?" (Notice any emotions present)

❑ "What's building?" (Notice what's getting stronger or fading)

❑ "What's blocking my view?" (Notice what thoughts keep circling)

Don't try to fix or change anything you notice. If anxiety is running high, simply note it. If sadness is present, acknowledge it. If your thoughts keep spinning about that work presentation, notice that too. The power isn't in having everything feel perfect—it's in knowing where you are, moment by moment, with honesty and openness.

This kind of self-awareness is a good, safe, and steady foundation; a safe place for you to land. Without it, you're navigating blind. With it, you can move through your day with clarity, even when the path ahead feels uncertain.

Acceptance is many things: it is opening your hands when they want to clench into fists. It is letting the tide of emotion wash through you instead of building walls against it. It is making room for the messy, imperfect reality of being human instead of chasing some airbrushed version of life.

Acceptance is looking at anxiety and saying "I see you." It's feeling sadness without rushing to fix it. It's allowing joy without waiting for the other shoe to drop. It's standing in the middle of uncertainty and keeping your heart open anyway.

Now, I want you to take your hand and place it against the steady rhythm of your heartbeat. Feel that constant pulse, that rhythm that's been with you since before you drew your first breath. Let these words sink in with each beat:

Acceptance is my word for the week. I will accept that some days will feel heavy and others will feel light. I will accept that my mind might race with worries, and that's okay. I will accept that healing isn't linear, and that courage often looks like simply staying present when I want to run. In the next chapter, we'll learn how emotional regulation teaches us to accept that we are exactly where we need to be right now, learning what we need to learn.

Chapter Three

MINDFULNESS FOR EMOTIONAL REGULATION

There's a story about a monk who lived beside a rushing river. Each morning, he would sit and watch as leaves, sticks, and debris flowed past. One day, a visitor came by and asked, "Why do you waste time watching garbage float by?" The monk smiled and said, "I'm not watching the garbage. I'm learning how everything, even the heaviest logs, eventually move on if you don't try to stop it."

Our emotions work like that river. We often think mindfulness means sitting cross-legged in perfect peace, emptying our minds of all thought. But real mindfulness is messier, and more dynamic. It's about learning to stay present as anxiety surges, as anger burns, as sadness weighs heavy.

I remember my first panic attack in a crowded subway car. My therapist had talked about mindfulness, but in that moment, all her serene instructions felt useless. My heart raced, sweat beaded on my forehead, and my mind screamed for escape. Then I remembered something simple: I could feel my feet on the floor. That one point of contact became my anchor, not to stop the panic, but to help me move through it.

This is what we'll explore—not how to achieve perfect calm, but how to stay present when emotions run high. Not how to empty your mind, but how to ground yourself in the middle of the storm.

UNDERSTANDING EMOTIONAL WAVES

Some days start okay. The world feels manageable, morning light feels gentle, and even traffic doesn't bother you. Then something shifts-a missed text, an awkward comment, or sometimes nothing at all. A wave of anxiety rises from nowhere. Your heart speeds up, thoughts race, and that sense of calm slips away.

Emotions move through us like this; it isn't in any neat patterns, but in waves that build, peak, and always subside. Our job isn't to control these waves but to learn how to stay afloat when they rise, knowing that no wave lasts forever.

The Science of Emotional Responses

Our emotions follow a clear path through our bodies. When something triggers us, our nervous system jumps into action within milliseconds. Our heart rate shifts, muscles tense, and breathing changes; all before we even realize what we feel.

Fighting these responses backfires. Push against anxiety, and stress hormones flood your system. Try to stop sadness, and it grows stronger. This happens because our bodies know how to process emotions naturally if we let them.

Each emotional wave typically lasts about 90 seconds if we don't resist it. But when we fight our feelings, that brief wave can stretch into hours or days. Our bodies designed this emotional system to protect us, not harm us.

Understanding this science helps us work with our emotions instead of against them. We learn to ride the waves rather than trying to stop them, knowing our nervous system will return to balance if we allow it.

GROUNDING TECHNIQUES

Grounding is derived from the physics concept of electrical grounding, which means connecting something to the earth to ensure safety and stability. In mental health, it serves a similar purpose. When emotions overwhelm us, when thoughts spin out of control, when anxiety pulls us into past regrets or future fears, grounding techniques anchor us back to the present moment.

Most people think grounding means forcing yourself to be calm, but it doesn't. Grounding is about finding steady ground when your internal world feels chaotic. It's like putting your feet on a solid floor when the room is spinning. Not to make the spinning stop, but to give yourself a reference point as it moves through you.

Research shows that connecting with our physical senses interrupts the stress response in our nervous system. When we feel the weight of our body in a chair, notice the texture of fabric under our fingers, or focus on specific sounds around us, we give our overwhelmed mind something concrete to hold onto.

The 5-4-3-2-1 Method

The 5-4-3-2-1 Method serves as a powerful anchor when your mind feels untethered. It works by systematically engaging each of your senses, pulling your attention away from overwhelming thoughts or feelings and back into your body. The key lies in its structured approach-moving from sight, which typically feels easiest to engage with, down to taste, which requires more focused attention.

Here's the detailed practice:

❑ **Start with FIVE things you can SEE:** Don't just glance around. Really look. Notice the way the light hits your coffee mug. The pattern on your colleague's shirt. The small crack in the ceiling you never noticed before. The way leaves move in the wind outside your window. The texture of your own skin. Be specific. Instead of "chair," notice "the worn spot on the armrest where my elbow always rests."

❑ **Find FOUR things you can TOUCH:** Run your fingers over different surfaces. Feel the smooth coolness of your desk. The rough texture of your jeans. The soft give of your chair cushion. The ridges on your phone case. Notice temperature, pressure, and texture. Is it smooth or rough? Warm or cool? Soft or hard?

❑ **Listen for THREE SOUNDS:** Close your eyes if that helps. What's the closest sound you hear? Maybe your own breathing or the hum of your computer. What's the farthest sound? Perhaps traffic outside or voices down the hall. What's a middle-distance sound? The ticking of a clock or the whir of air conditioning.

❑ **Identify TWO SMELLS:** This one might take more attention. Maybe you notice your morning coffee, hand lotion, the leather of your chair, or simply the clean smell of air. If you can't find two distinct smells, that's okay. The act of searching still engages your brain in the present moment.

❑ **Focus on ONE TASTE:** Notice what's already in your mouth. Is there a lingering taste from your last meal? The mint from your toothpaste? If not, take a sip of water or touch your tongue to the roof of your mouth. Notice any subtle flavors or sensations.

The technique is efficient because it's so thorough. By the time you reach "taste," your mind has been thoroughly redirected from whatever was overwhelming it. Your nervous system has shifted from fight-or-flight back to a state of present awareness.

Physical Anchors

Your body isn't just along for the ride during intense emotions—it's your most reliable tool for finding stability. When your mind races or anxiety spikes, these physical techniques work by activating your body's natural calming system.

❑ **Feet to Floor:** Plant your feet firmly on the ground. Push down through your heels, then your arches, then your toes. Notice how the solid surface pushes back. This connection with the ground triggers your body's sense of physical stability, which can help regulate your emotional state.

❑ **Cold Water Reset:** Running cold water over your wrists isn't just refreshing—it triggers your diving reflex, a physiological response that naturally slows your heart rate and calms your breathing. Hold your wrists under the stream for 30-60 seconds, noticing the sensation of cold against your pulse points.

❑ **Weight and Pressure:** Heavy objects activate your body's proprioceptive system-your sense of where you are in space. Hold a heavy book against your chest. Feel its weight. Squeeze a stress ball or press your palms together firmly. This pressure sends signals to your brain that help anchor you in the present moment.

❑ **Texture Focus:** Keep something with a distinctive texture in your pocket—a smooth stone, a rough piece of bark, or a soft fabric. When emotions run high, touch it with purpose. Notice every ridge, bump, or smooth spot. This sensory input helps redirect your attention from internal chaos to external sensation.

Quick Resets

Sometimes you need an immediate way to steady yourself. These techniques work in under a minute, making them perfect for moments when emotions surge unexpectedly during a meeting, in traffic, or in the middle of a conversation.

❑ **Belly Breathing Reset**: Place one hand on your chest and one on your belly. Breathe slowly so your belly hand rises while your chest hand stays still. This engages your diaphragm, activating your vagus nerve which regulates your stress response. Take three breaths this way, making each exhale longer than the inhale.

❑ **Progressive Muscle Release:** Start with your toes. Curl them tight, hold for five seconds, then release completely. Move to your feet, then calves, working up to your face. This systematic tension and release interrupt the stress cycle in your body and releases built-up physical tension.

❑ **Mental Redirects:** These cognitive tasks engage your prefrontal cortex, pulling attention away from emotional overwhelm:

  ❑ Start at 100, subtract 7 repeatedly (100, 93, 86...)

  ❑ Name objects alphabetically ("apple, book, chair...")

  ❑ Describe your surroundings in detail, focusing on facts ("The wall is white, the chair is leather, the table has four legs...")

The key is to practice these when you're calm so they become automatic when you need them most.

Tracking Your Grounding Practice

After trying these grounding techniques, you need a way to understand what works best for you. Different methods work better in different situations, and keeping track helps you build a reliable toolkit for when anxiety, OCD, or overwhelm strikes.

The tracker helps you map out which of the techniques serve you best and when. This isn't about judging success or failure—it's about gathering information that makes your practice more effective over time.

This is how you use the tracker:

❑ Write down the date and time you use a grounding technique

❑ Note which method you chose (5-4-3-2-1, Physical Anchors, Quick Resets)

❑ Rate your distress level before and after (1-10 scale)

❑ Note where you were and what triggered the need for grounding Add brief notes about what worked or didn't

Here is an example entry:

DATE	Tuesday 10 am
SITUATION	Work presentation anxiety
METHOD	5-4-3-2-1
BEFORE	8/10 distress AFTER 5/10 distress
NOTES	Helped most when I focused extra time on sounds

Keep your tracker visible and easy to access. Fill it out as soon as you can after using a technique while the experience remains fresh. Over time, patterns will emerge showing you exactly what helps in specific situations.

BUILDING A DAILY PRACTICE

I learned how to ride a bike when I was twenty-two. Not the most graceful beginning; as there was lots of wobbling, a few falls, and more than a few moments of wondering if I'd ever get it. But here's what stuck with me: it wasn't the long practice sessions that finally made it click. It was the small moments of getting it right—three seconds of balance here, five seconds of smooth pedaling there.

Building a mindfulness practice works the same way. It's not about marathon meditation sessions or achieving some perfect state of calm. It's about collecting small moments of awareness throughout your day, until they start to add up to something bigger.

Small Moments Matter

Small moments hold the biggest weight. That first sip of morning coffee, the pause between meetings, the walk to your car; these ordinary moments become doorways to presence when we learn to notice them. Like water smoothing stones in a river, it's the consistent touch of attention that gradually shapes how we experience our lives.

These brief pauses matter more than long sessions of formal practice because they weave awareness into the fabric of daily life. You don't need special equipment or extra time. You don't need perfect silence or a quiet room. All you need is the willingness to notice what's already happening: the sensation of your feet on the floor, the rhythm of your breath, the play of sunlight through your window.

The real power lies in repetition, not duration. Each time you pause to notice your breath while waiting for the elevator, each moment you feel your hands on the steering wheel at a red light, each brief check-in while your computer boots up—you're strengthening your capacity to stay present. These small practices build resilience for bigger moments, like muscles developing through regular use.

Piggyback on Existing Habits

Piggybacking is a concept that explains how new habits stick better when attached to existing ones. Every day has dozens of automatic moments; things you do without thinking twice. These become your anchors.

Here's how it works:

Pick one reliable action, something you do every day without fail, like unlocking your phone or starting your car. Add one tiny moment of awareness to this action. When you unlock your phone, take three breaths before opening any apps. When you start your car, feel your hands on the wheel for five seconds before driving.

Start small and specific. Don't try to overhaul your whole morning routine at once. Choose one trigger and one small addition. Once that feels natural, like after a week or so, add another. The power lies in choosing triggers that already have a permanent place in your day. Your existing habits do the heavy lifting; you just add a small note of awareness to what's already there.

At the end of the day, consistency beats ambition. A three-second pause you actually do is worth more than a ten-minute practice you skip.

Creating Personal Anchors

Your personal anchors are the things that already punctuate your day; in other words: the coffee or cup of tea that you make, the doorways you pass through, the sound of your car starting.

These ordinary moments can become powerful reminders to pause and notice where you are.

A colored dot on your bathroom mirror catches your eye each morning. The lock screen on your phone shows a simple word or image. Your office threshold marks a boundary between spaces. Each of these becomes a bell, calling you back to your body, your breath, the present moment.

You want to choose anchors that you'll actually encounter, not aspirational ones. That plant on your desk is a better reminder than a meditation app you'll never open. The sound of your computer starting works better than an alarm you'll learn to ignore. Keep your anchors simple, visible, and tied to your actual daily patterns.

These small practices build resilience for bigger emotional challenges. Like building muscle through regular exercise, daily mindful moments strengthen your ability to stay grounded when life gets tough.

If I asked you: when was the last time you breathed, what would you say to me? Most likely you'd pause, take a breath, and become suddenly aware of this automatic rhythm that's been with you since birth. That's what mindfulness offers—not some complex practice, but a simple return to what's already here. Your breath moves whether you notice it or not. Your senses take in the world whether you pay attention or not. All these practices do is invite you to show up for what's already happening. Let's now go and learn how values can connect us more deeply to who we are.

Chapter Four

UNDERSTANDING PERSONAL VALUES

My grandmother used to say that if you stand for nothing at all, you'll fall for everything. She wasn't a person that was big on lengthy advice or complex wisdom, just straight truths, that were usually delivered while kneading bread or folding laundry.

For years, I misunderstood what she meant, I thought having values meant having opinions, taking stands, drawing lines in the sand. But now I understand she was talking about something deeper; that internal compass that guides us when life gets complicated. The quiet knowing that helps us choose between what looks good and what feels right.

Most of us think we know our values. We say things like "family matters most," "health is important," or "integrity above all." But when life hands us real choices—a promotion that means less time at home, a friendship that asks us to compromise our principles, or a decision between security and growth; we realize that knowing our values and living them are two very different things.

UNDERSTANDING TRUE VALUES

Okay, the first thing I want you to understand is this: there's a very big difference between the values you inherit and the ones that you choose yourself. Think about the first time you made a major life decision that went against what everyone expected. Maybe you chose a different career path than your parents planned. Or moved to a city when everyone said to stay close to home. Or ended a relationship that looked perfect on paper but felt wrong in your gut.

These moments are what reveal the gap between inherited values, which are the "shoulds" that are passed down through family, culture, and society, and your true values. The inherited ones sound like "you should want stability," "you should prioritize status," or "you should settle down by now." They come packaged with well-meaning advice and societal norms.

However, beneath these external pressures lie your actual values—the ones that resonate in your bones when you're completely honest with yourself. These aren't about what you should want. They're about what moves you, what matters when no one's watching, what you'd choose if you knew no one would judge your choice.

Most of us live in the shadow of inherited values without realizing it because we chase careers we're supposed to want, maintain relationships we're supposed to value, and set goals we're supposed to have. Breaking free requires asking yourself hard questions: What would I choose if no one else's opinion mattered? What do I genuinely care about, separate from what I've been taught to care about?

VALUES VS. GOALS

Someone once asked me what the difference was between a goal and a value. I sat with that question for days. At first, they seemed the same—after all, don't we value what we aim for? But then I thought about my friend Sarah, who spent years chasing the goal of marriage. She achieved it, and checked that box, but still felt empty because what she really valued wasn't the certificate-it was deep connection, honesty, and growth together.

Values illuminate the path while goals mark spots along the way. Getting promoted is a goal; you either reach it or you don't.

But doing meaningful work is a value you can live by today, whether you're the CEO or just starting out. Running a marathon is a goal—it has a finish line. But caring for your health is a value you can honor with each choice you make.

When you confuse goals with values, you risk chasing destinations while missing the point of the journey. You might reach every goal and still feel lost if those achievements don't align with what truly matters to you.

COMMON VALUE AREAS

In every life, there are territories that matter—spaces where our choices shape not just what we do, but who we become. These aren't just categories on a list. They're the arenas where our values come alive through daily decisions.

Relationships:

Here's what matters in how we relate to others: Do we value depth or breadth? Some people light up in one-on-one conversations, diving deep into life's big questions. Others thrive on bringing people together, and creating communities and connections. It's about identifying your authentic way of connecting. When do you feel most real with others? What kind of presence do you want to be in people's lives?

Consider Mark, who spends every Sunday with his aging father, having long conversations over coffee, even when work deadlines loom. Or Sarah, who maintains three close friendships rather than a wide social circle, prioritizing intimate connection over networking.

Work and Career:

Work isn't just about earning—it's about contribution. What problems do you want to solve? Some find purpose in nurturing others' growth through teaching or mentoring. Others value innovation, pushing boundaries of what's possible. Some prioritize stability and expertise, becoming masters of their craft.

Lisa turned down a management position to keep teaching third grade because she values direct impact over status. Or James, who chose freelancing over a stable corporate job because he values autonomy more than security.

Personal Growth:

This is a form of self-expression. What parts of yourself are asking to be developed? Maybe you value creative expression, turning inner visions into reality. Or perhaps you're drawn to understanding—always learning, questioning, exploring.

Like Miguel, who spends his evenings learning languages instead of watching TV because he values continuous learning. Or Rachel, who takes dance classes not to perform, but because she values creative expression and being a beginner at something new.

Health and Wellbeing:

Your relationship with health reveals deep values. Some value endurance-testing their limits, and pushing boundaries. Others prioritize balance-finding sustainable ways to thrive. Some focus on a mindful connection with their body.

Consider David, who chooses morning runs not for weight loss but because he values the mental clarity it brings. Or Ana, who practices yoga not for flexibility but because she values the mind-body connection it creates.

Community and Contribution:

This is about your place in the larger story. What role do you want to play in your community? Some value being catalysts for change, while others prefer quiet, consistent support. Some build institutions, others nurture individual growth.

Like Karen, who despite a busy schedule, volunteers weekly at a literacy program because she values educational access. Or Tom, who grows vegetables in his front yard to share with neighbors because he values building community through small acts of generosity.

These choices, however big and small, paint a picture of what matters most to each person. They're not goals to achieve but ways of being that can guide every decision.

VALUES IN ACTION

Values become real when they meet life's hard moments. It's easy to say you value family until work demands collide with your child's school play. It's easy to claim you value health until you're choosing between sleep and meeting a deadline. The rubber meets the road when your values face real challenges.

Let's look at how this works in practice through real situations. When facing a difficult colleague at work, your immediate instinct might be avoidance or confrontation. But if you value professional growth and compassion, your approach shifts. Instead of firing off an angry email, you might take a breath and ask, "What would acting from my values look like here?" Maybe you initiate that uncomfortable conversation, acknowledging both perspectives. Maybe you set clear, professional boundaries while maintaining respect. Your values become your compass, pointing toward growth rather than reaction.

Here's a common scenario: Your friend's startup needs help, and they've asked you to take on a major role. You want to be supportive, but you're already stretched thin with your own projects. If you value both loyalty and authenticity, this becomes a moment of truth. Acting from your values might mean having an honest conversation about what you can realistically offer, rather than making promises you can't keep.

Take a family situation: Your teenager wants more independence, but you value both their safety and their growth. Instead of just saying no or giving in, your values guide you toward a more nuanced response. Maybe you work together to build trust gradually, setting small tests of responsibility that honor both protection and growth.

Putting values into action starts with naming your challenge with absolute clarity. Not just "I'm stuck" but "I'm avoiding difficult conversations with my partner because I'm afraid of conflict." Next, identify the values at stake—usually there are several competing ones like connection and safety, truth and kindness, growth and stability.

Then envision what acting from these values might look like. Ask yourself what small step would move you toward rather than away from what matters. Choose one action that expresses your values, whether that's having that difficult conversation you've been avoiding or setting a boundary that feels both kind and clear.

After taking action, reflect on how it aligned with your values. What did you learn about what matters most to you? How can you build on this step? Remember: Values-based action isn't about perfection. It's about making conscious choices, one situation at a time, that reflect who you want to be.

NAVIGATING VALUE CONFLICTS

Value conflicts hit at our core because there's often no clear "right" choice. When your value of career growth collides with your commitment to family, or when financial security clashes with pursuing meaningful work, you're not choosing between right and wrong—you're choosing between competing "rights."

Here's how to navigate these crossroads:

First, recognize that values exist on a spectrum, not as absolutes. Maybe you can't be at every family dinner, but you can make the ones you attend fully present. You might not be able to take every creative risk at work, but you can find smaller ways to express innovation within security.

Sometimes the conflict comes from treating values as all-or-nothing. Take health versus achievement: Instead of working late every night or never working late, you might set clear boundaries about which nights you'll extend your work and which are non-negotiable for rest.

The hardest conflicts often involve different life domains: personal versus professional, individual versus collective, and short-term versus long-term. A promotion might align with your value of professional growth but conflict with your value of work-life balance. During these times, ask yourself: "Which choice will I respect myself for making five years from now? Which aligns with my deepest values, not just my immediate pressures?"

The key is to make these choices consciously, understanding that perfect solutions rarely exist. Sometimes you'll need to disappoint people you respect. Sometimes you'll need to sit with the discomfort of not fully honoring every value. What matters is making these choices deliberately, with an awareness of your deeper priorities.

You have the values that you have right now, but you're human, and you're changing, which means that your values might shift too. What mattered most in your twenties might look different in your forties. What seemed crucial last year might feel less important today. This isn't weakness or inconsistency-it's growth.

Let your values breathe and evolve with you. Check in with them regularly. Ask yourself: "Does this still matter to me? Why?" Sometimes what changes isn't the core value itself but how you express it. The way you show love at twenty-five might look different at fifty. The way you pursue growth might shift as your life circumstances change.

Values aren't a fixed destination you reach once and for all. They're a living compass that grows with you, helping you navigate each new chapter of your life with intention and authenticity.

EXPLORING YOUR VALUES: A WORKSHEET

Before we tackle these questions, find a quiet moment where you won't feel rushed. Keep a pen handy because sometimes values reveal themselves in sudden insights. What you write here will likely shift and evolve as you work through it—let it be messy, let it be real.

You might discover that some answers surprise you, that what you genuinely value differs from what you thought. Welcome these surprises. They often point toward your truest path. And remember, there are no right or wrong answers here—only honest ones.

As you move through each section, notice which questions energize you and which ones make you want to skip ahead. Both reactions tell you something important about what matters to you.

Part 1: Mapping Inherited Values

Think about messages you received growing up about what matters in life. Write down:

❑ What your family said "success" looks like

❑ What your culture values most highly

❑ What society tells you to prioritize

❑ The "shoulds" that echo in your mind

For example:

❑ "I should own a house by 30"

❑ "A good career means climbing the corporate ladder"

❑ "Family always comes before personal goals"

Part 2: Finding Your True Values

Remember specific moments when you felt most alive or proud of your choices. Write about:

A time you made a decision that others questioned but felt right to you:

❑ What was the situation?

❑ Why did you choose differently?

❑ How did it align with what matters to you?

A moment when you felt completely yourself:

❑ What were you doing?

❑ Who were you with (if anyone)?

❑ What made this moment meaningful?

Part 3: Values in Daily Life

Pick three areas where you notice the tension between inherited and true values:

Example: Career

❑ Inherited value: "Status and salary define success"

❑ Your true value: "Creating work that helps others"

❑ Real-life example: "Choosing to teach instead of pursuing law"

Area 1:

❑ Inherited value: _____

❑ Your true value: _____

❑ Real-life example: _____

Area 2:

❑ Inherited value: _____

❑ Your true value: _____

❑ Real-life example: _____

Area 3:

❑ Inherited value: _____

❑ Your true value: _____

❑ Real-life example: _____

Part 4: Moving Forward

Choose one area where you want to align more with your true values:

Area ---

What small step could you take this week?

What support do you need?

What might get in your way?

How will you respond to resistance?

Keep this worksheet visible. Return to it when you face decisions or feel pulled between different values. Use it to remind yourself what truly matters to you.

We will be who we are at different points in our lives. We will change and not change and then change some more again, but nonetheless, what matters is that we stay connected to the thread of what moves us, what lights us up, and what makes our lives feel meaningful.

Living by your values isn't about reaching some final destination. There's no graduation ceremony, no finish line to cross. Instead, there's the quiet victory of choosing kindness when anger would be easier. The small triumph of staying true to yourself when pressure mounts to conform. The daily practice of turning toward what matters, even when the path seems unclear.

In the next chapter, we learn that each choice you make today becomes part of the story you're living. Not the story others expect you to live, or the story you think you should live, but the one that feels true in your bones. Let that truth guide you forward.

Chapter Five

TAKING ACTION ON YOUR VALUES

It's okay to want what you want; in fact, it's more than okay, it's essential. We spend so much time questioning our desires, doubting our direction, wondering if we're choosing the "right" path. But here's the truth: values aren't about right or wrong. They're about what lights you up, what matters in your bones, and what you want to stand for in this one wildlife.

I used to think taking action on values meant making big, dramatic changes. Quitting your job. Ending relationships. Moving across the country. But real change happens in small moments, in tiny choices that add up over time. It's choosing to listen fully when someone speaks, even when you're busy. It's taking that walk at lunch because you value health. It's speaking up in a meeting because you value authenticity.

These moments might seem insignificant on their own, but each one is like a vote for the person you want to become, the life you want to create. Each small choice shapes the path you're walking.

FROM THINKING TO DOING

Values become solidified when we choose to act differently in familiar situations. The gap between knowing our values and living them appears in daily choices; that is how we handle stress, respond to others, or approach challenges.

Let's make this real by being present. The moment arrives after work; your mind races with deadlines while your partner asks about your day. Right here, in how you handle the next few minutes, your values either come alive or remain just ideas. One small shift, like putting away your phone and truly listening, turns your value from concept to reality.

You don't need perfect conditions or dramatic changes. Values live in these everyday moments where you choose to respond differently. This is how values move from ideas in your head to changes in your life.

BUILDING DAILY PRACTICES

I love mornings. I love that brief pocket of time before the world fully wakes, when possibilities feel fresh, and choices haven't yet been made. For years, I'd stumble through these precious hours, rushing to check emails or scrolling through the news. Now, mornings serve as my anchor for values-based living.

Here's how to build practices that keep you connected to your values throughout the day:

Morning Check-in:

Start with your first cup of coffee or tea, before emails or news. This moment sets your internal compass for the day ahead. Place both feet on the floor, feel the warmth of your cup in your hands, and take three slow breaths.

Ask yourself: "What matters most today?" Not what's most urgent or what others expect, but what truly matters to you. Maybe it's being fully present with your team. Maybe it's bringing creativity to a challenging project. Maybe it's maintaining balance amid pressure.

Then go deeper: "How do I want to show up?" This isn't about performance or perfection. It's about intention. If you value courage, maybe today that means speaking up in the big meeting. If you value growth, perhaps it's about staying curious when facing criticism.

Notice which values feel particularly important for the day ahead. Some days might call for patience, others for determination. Let these values become your anchors, quiet reminders you can return to when the day gets challenging.

This practice takes five minutes, but it can reshape your entire day. It's not about adding another task to your morning—it's about bringing consciousness to a moment you already have.

Mindful Transitions:

Use everyday moments as value checkpoints. Your commute, walking between meetings, waiting in line—these become opportunities to reconnect with what matters.

Decision Filters:

When a decision comes up, be it a quick email response or a major life choice, pause for a moment. Take a breath. This small gap between stimulus and response is where your values can speak.

Ask yourself three key questions:

- ❑ Which choice aligns with who I want to be, not just what I want to achieve?
- ❑ What would this decision look like through the lens of my core values?
- ❑ Will this choice move me toward or away from what matters most?

This filter works for both big and small decisions. When choosing how to spend your evening, check which option better serves your values. If you value health and connection, maybe it's choosing a walk with your partner over another hour of work. If facing a difficult conversation, let your values of honesty and compassion guide your words.

You don't always have to make the perfect choice because you won't always, but what you can will yourself to do is to make conscious choices because sometimes you'll choose against your values for practical reasons. The key is knowing you're making that choice deliberately, not by default.

Let me create a practical decision filter worksheet:

DECISION FILTER WORKSHEET

This worksheet guides you through filtering choices through your values. It is like creating a conversation between your immediate reactions and your deeper wisdom. Use it when you feel torn between options, when a choice nags at you, or when you want to make sure you're moving in a direction that truly fits who you are.

Take a moment now to think of a decision you currently face. It doesn't have to be huge, sometimes practicing with smaller choices helps us prepare for bigger ones. Let's work through it together.

Step 1: Clarify Your Choice

Write down the decision you face right now:

List the options in front of you:

Note your immediate gut reaction:

Step 2: Values Check

Which values come into play with this decision?

Value 1: _____

How does this option support or conflict with it?

Value 2: _____

How does this option support or conflict with it?

Value 3: _____

How does this option support or conflict with it?

Step 3: Future Impact

How will this choice affect:

The next few days:

The next few months:

A year from now:

Step 4: Reality Check

What practical constraints exist?

What resources do you have available?

What support might you need?

Step 5: Decision Clarity

On a scale of 1-10:

❑ How well does this align with your values? _____

❑ How practical is this choice right now? _____

❑ How will you feel about this choice looking back?_____

Not every decision is going to perfectly align with all your values, just note which values you're choosing to prioritize in this moment and why.

Evening Reflection:

Before your head hits the pillow, take a quiet moment, just you and your thoughts. This isn't about judging your day or making lists for tomorrow. It's about noticing with honesty and kindness where your actions and values meet.

Ask yourself: "When did I act in line with what matters most today?" Maybe you showed patience during a tough meeting, or chose honesty in a difficult moment, or made time for what truly matters despite the pressure to do otherwise.

Then consider: "Where did I miss opportunities to express my values?" Not to blame yourself, but to learn something. Maybe you come to a realization that you rushed through a conversation when you value connection, or that you stayed silent when you value courage. These aren't failures-they're information about tomorrow's choices.

Finally, let yourself notice one specific moment when your actions and values align perfectly. Hold onto that feeling. Let it be the last thing you consider before sleep, a reminder of who you're becoming, one choice at a time.

Tracking and Learning

For the last couple of weeks, I have sat down with my notebook and looked back at seven days of choices. Some moments, like the time I chose patience with my daughter despite a looming deadline, and the moment I spoke up in a meeting when silence felt safer, were clearly noticeable, and other moments showed me where I'd drifted from what matters most.

Start with simple notation. At the end of each week, take ten minutes to reflect. Where did your actions align with your values? Maybe you chose to listen deeply when a friend was struggling, even though you were busy. Maybe you spoke up in a meeting despite your fear. Notice these moments to understand your patterns.

Pay attention to what stands between you and your values. Often it's awareness rather than commitment that makes the difference. You might observe that your values take a back seat when you're tired, rushed, or feeling insecure. These moments offer valuable information about where you need more support or different strategies.

Watch for the bright spots—those moments when living your values felt natural and rewarding. What made those moments possible? Perhaps you were well-rested, or had support, or had prepared in advance. These successes leave clues about how to make values-based choices more consistent.

When setbacks happen (which they will) treat them as data. Each time you act against your values, ask yourself: "What was happening here? What did I need in that moment?" The goal focuses on learning and adjusting as you go.

Remember: This process helps you understand your life better. Each choice, whether aligned with your values or not, teaches you something about what you need to live more fully as the person you want to be.

Overcoming Common Obstacles

They say that you need to stay calm under pressure, manage your time better, and find balance. Easy advice to give, harder to follow when you're racing to meet a deadline, your phone won't stop buzzing, and your energy is running on fumes.

❑ **Time Pressure:** This is often the first thing to derail our values. When deadlines loom and demands pile up, we default to efficiency over meaning. You might skip the morning check-in with your partner because you're running late, or cut corners on a project when you value quality work. Time pressure tricks us into believing we can't afford to live by our values, when actually, we can't afford not to.

❑ **Energy management:** Your energy affects everything; how you react, how you choose, how you show up. Low-energy days make it tempting to take the path of least resistance rather than the path of value. You might skip that difficult but important conversation because you're tired, or choose mindless scrolling over meaningful connection. Understanding your energy patterns helps you plan when to tackle challenges that align with your values.

❑ **Competing priorities:** Life rarely presents clean, clear choices. More often, you're juggling multiple important things: family needs, work demands, and personal well-being. Your value of being a present parent competes with your value of professional excellence. Your need for rest conflicts with your desire to help others. These aren't problems to solve but tensions to navigate.

❑ **Stress response:** Under stress, we typically revert to old patterns rather than living by our chosen values. Your body tenses, your mind narrows, and suddenly survival feels more important than growth or connection. The key is recognizing these stress responses early and having simple practices ready-like three deep breaths or feeling your feet on the floor to help you stay grounded in your values even when stressed.

Moving Forward

A small step forward is better than no step at all. I watched my niece in her first dance recital. She forgot half the steps, and moved in the wrong direction several times, but kept her eyes bright and her feet moving. In the end, she didn't focus on what went wrong-she was too busy feeling proud of simply being on that stage.

Living our values works just like that sometimes, it's about staying in motion, keeping your eyes on what matters, and finding your own rhythm. Some days you'll nail the routine. Other days you'll step on your own feet. Both are part of the dance.

Think about how athletes build strength. They don't start with their maximum weight. They begin where they are, gradually increasing as their capacity grows. Your values muscle works the same way. Start with manageable moments—speaking one truth, showing one kindness, taking one brave step. Let these moments build on each other.

The path forward isn't about dramatic transformations. It's about becoming fluent in your own values language. Like learning any language, you'll fumble at first. You'll make mistakes. You'll have days when the words flow naturally and days when they feel stuck in your throat. Keep practicing anyway.

WEEKLY VALUES ALIGNMENT TRACKER

This simple tracker helps you notice how your actions match your values each day. It's not about scoring perfect marks but about building awareness and making adjustments as you go. Fill it out briefly each evening, noting moments that stand out.

MONDAY

DATE _ _ _ _ _ _ _ _ _ _ _ _ _ _ _

Action taken:

_____

_____

Value it served: _____

What worked:

_____

_____

What I learned:

_____

_____

TUESDAY

DATE _ _ _ _ _ _ _ _ _ _ _ _ _ _ _

Action taken:

_____

_____

Value it served: _____

What worked:

_____

_____

What I learned:

_____

_____

WEDNESDAY   DATE _____

Action taken:

Value it served: _____

What worked:

What I learned:

THURSDAY   DATE _____

Action taken:

Value it served: _____

What worked:

What I learned:

FRIDAY

DATE ----------------

Action taken:

Value it served: --

What worked:

What I learned:

SATURDAY

DATE ----------------

Action taken:

Value it served: --

What worked:

What I learned:

SUNDAY   DATE _____

Action taken:

_____

_____

Value it served: _____

What worked:

_____

_____

What I learned:

_____

_____

WEEKLY REFLECTION   DATE _____

Values that showed up most:

_____

_____

Challenging moments:

_____

_____

_____

_____

_____

_____

Proud moments:

Focus for next week:

QUICK TIPS:

❏ Write down specific actions, not general ideas

❏ Note both easy and difficult moments

❏ Include small choices that mattered

❏ Track what learned, not just what you did

We will be who we are at different points in our lives. We will change and not change and then change some more again, but nonetheless, what matters is that we stay connected to the thread of what moves us, what lights us up, and what makes our lives feel meaningful.

Living by your values isn't about reaching some final destination. There's no graduation ceremony, no finish line to cross. Instead, there's the quiet victory of choosing kindness when anger would be easier. The small triumph of staying true to yourself when pressure mounts to conform. The daily practice of turning toward what matters, even when the path seems unclear.

Each choice you make today becomes part of the story you're living. Not the story others expect you to live, or the story you think you should live, but the one that feels true in your bones. Let that truth guide you forward.

Conclusion

The human heart is as elastic as can be. It stretches to hold joy alongside sorrow, courage alongside fear, and growth alongside uncertainty. This elasticity isn't weakness-it's what allows us to fully experience life in all its complexity.

Through this workbook, you've explored how ACT's core processes work together: acceptance helps you meet difficult feelings with openness, defusion creates space around sticky thoughts, and while mindfulness grounds you in the present moment. You've discovered the self as a perspective of possibility, values as guides when the path feels unclear, and committed action as the way forward even when doubt shows up.

True well-being comes from building psychological flexibility—staying present, opening up to experiences, and doing what matters most in the midst of challenges. You can live fully while anxiety exists. You can take meaningful action before perfect clarity arrives.

This is the heart of ACT-learning to free yourself and live with purpose. Building your capacity to embrace experience while moving toward what matters most. Moving forward with life's challenges, through them, and because of them as part of your human experience.

Let this be your foundation for living-fully present, deeply engaged, and moving toward what matters most.

Book Two

MINDFULNESS AND RADICAL ACCEPTANCE

Science-Backed Stress Management
Techniques to Find Peace and Balance

Introduction

There's a story about two men at a train station. One paces anxiously, checking his watch repeatedly as the train runs two minutes late. The other sits quietly reading, undisturbed by the delay. Same situation, vastly different experiences.

This moment captures how we meet life's challenges. Some situations will bring delays, others disappointments, and some will overflow with unexpected joy. Our response to these moments shapes our experience more than the moments themselves. Just like those two men at the station, each of us has developed our own patterns for handling stress and uncertainty.

Take a moment now to think about your own patterns. When you last faced an unexpected delay or change of plans:

❑ What physical sensations showed up first?

❑ Which thoughts immediately took over?

❑ How did you respond?

❑ What happened next?

This book opens the door to a different way of being—one where you learn to stay steady when things go wrong, and where you find ease amid imperfection. It offers practical tools to help you meet all of life's moments with more space and understanding.

Chapter One
UNDERSTANDING STRESS

Stress is that moment when everything speeds up and slows down at the same time. Your heart races, your mind freezes, and somehow everything and nothing seems urgent. It's the morning when your alarm doesn't go off, the email that can't wait, the phone call you've been dreading.

We feel stress in our bodies-in tight shoulders and shallow breaths. We feel it in our minds—in spinning thoughts and midnight worries. It lives in the gap between what life demands and what we believe we can handle.

Your body knows stress intimately. Right now, as you read these words, you might notice tension in your jaw, a slight holding in your stomach, and a tightness in your chest. These sensations tell a story—not just about this moment, but about how you've learned to move through a world that often asks too much.

Stress serves as a natural response to life's demands, a response that's been keeping humans alive and alert for thousands of years. Like an ancient alarm system wired into our DNA, it warns us, protects us, and motivates us. Yet in our modern world, this survival mechanism often gets stuck in the 'on' position.

THE BIOLOGICAL FOUNDATION OF STRESS

Your body responds to stress through a clear biological chain reaction. When you face a challenging situation, like giving an important presentation, your brain's alarm center signals danger. Your adrenal glands release stress hormones-adrenaline and cortisol-triggering immediate physical changes. Your heart pounds to send blood to your muscles, your breathing quickens to fuel your brain, and your muscles tighten to prepare for action.

This stress response leads to three possible reactions: fight (pushing through despite anxiety), flight (avoiding the situation), or freeze (becoming still until danger passes). While this reaction helped our ancestors survive predators, today it shows up during work deadlines and difficult conversations. When these responses trigger repeatedly, they can leave you feeling drained and on edge, your body always prepared for a threat that never arrives.

YOUR MIND UNDER STRESS

Stress changes how your brain processes information, like trying to write a coherent email while multiple alarms blast around you. When stress floods your brain with survival chemicals, simple tasks become puzzling. Your thoughts scatter, your focus drops, and even familiar activities feel strangely complex.

Your emotional landscape shifts dramatically because your mind amplifies threats and minimizes resources. Small irritations grow into major provocations while normal challenges transform into impossible barriers. These thought patterns emerge predictably, warping your perception until you see threats where none exist. When you notice these changes, you can start to recognize them as temporary shifts in your brain's processing rather than reflections of reality.

MANAGING AND MITIGATING STRESS EFFECTIVELY

My grandmother was a storyteller at heart, and she used to say that fighting against a river's current would only exhaust you. "Learn to swim with the water," she'd tell me, "and you'll find the river becomes your guide instead of your enemy."

The same wisdom applies to stress. Most of us spend years treating stress as something to conquer, eliminate, or overcome. We tense against it, push back against it, and try to control it. But just like fighting the river, this approach often leaves us more exhausted than when we started.

Stress speaks to us through our bodies and minds, offering valuable information if we learn to listen. When a deadline looms and our shoulders tense, it tells us to adjust our schedule. When anxiety spikes in social situations, it points to our need for deeper connections. When tension builds at work, it signals the time for an honest conversation.

This shift in perspective doesn't make stress comfortable or pleasant. It doesn't ask us to accept being overwhelmed. Rather, it invites us to listen to what stress tells us, understand its messages, and respond with wisdom rather than reaction.

Practice in Low-Stakes Moments Most people wait until they're overwhelmed to work with stress. This is like trying to learn to swim in a storm. Instead, use daily irritations as your training ground. When someone cuts you off in traffic or your computer runs slow, notice your automatic reactions. Feel where the tension lives in your body. Watch how your thoughts spiral. These seemingly minor moments teach you about your stress patterns when the stakes are low.

Here are some tips to work with, instead of against your stress.

❑ **Read your body's language:** Your neck tightens during certain conversations. Your stomach knots before specific meetings. Your shoulders climb toward your ears when checking email.

These physical responses aren't random—they're your body's early warning system. Track these sensations for a week. Write them down. Patterns will emerge, showing you exactly where and how stress first appears in your life.

❑ **Meet Stress Differently:** When stress rises, most of us either fight it or run from it. We tense against it or try to distract ourselves. Try this instead: Next time stress hits, turn toward it with curiosity. Notice its texture, its temperature, and its shape. Where does it live in your body? How does it move? This isn't about making stress go away—it's about changing your relationship with it.

❑ **Transform your understanding:** Stress often carries messages we need to hear. That overwhelm at work might be telling you it's time to delegate, and that anxiety in relationships might be showing you where you need stronger boundaries. That constant tension might be pointing toward necessary changes. Learn to ask: "What is this stress trying to tell me?"

❑ **Let stress guide growth:** Stress is like an internal navigation system, pointing toward areas in your life that need attention. When you feel stressed about speaking up in meetings, it might be highlighting the need to develop your voice. When family conflicts create tension, it might be showing you where relationships need tending. Use stress as a flashlight, illuminating places for potential growth.

MAPPING YOUR STRESS RESPONSE: A WORKSHEET

Track your stress reactions over the next week. Notice what triggers your stress response and how your body and mind respond. Be specific about situations and sensations.

Situation 1

Trigger (What happened?): _____
_____

Time/Place: _____

Physical Responses:

❑ Heart rate changes: _____

❑ Breathing patterns: _____

❑ Muscle tension spots: _____

❑ Other body sensations: _____

Thought Patterns:

❑ First thoughts: _____

❑ Stories your mind created: _____

❑ How your focus changed: _____

What You Did:

❑ Immediate reaction: _____

❑ What helped: _____

❑ What didn't help: _____

Repeat this pattern for 2-3 more situations, then reflect:

Common Patterns

Physical: Which body responses show up most often?

Mental: Which thought patterns repeat?

Behavioral: How do you typically react?

Key Insights

What did you learn about your stress signals?

Which responses feel most challenging?

What helps you steady yourself?

Use these observations to recognize your stress patterns early and respond more skillfully.

Exercise: Reading Your Stress Signals

So what is essentially happening when stress moves through us? We feel it in our bodies, we notice triggers in our environment, and we respond—often automatically, without conscious choice. To understand your own stress patterns better, I've designed a week-long mapping exercise. Think of it as creating a personal atlas of your stress landscape.

Take the next seven days to map your stress landscape. You'll need:

❑ A small notebook you can carry with you

❑ Five minutes each evening

❑ Your honest attention

Each day, track three things:

First: Physical Location Where do you feel stress in your body? Be specific. Instead of just noting "tension," write "jaw clenches during morning meetings" or "stomach tightens when checking email." Map these sensations like a detective gathering clues.

Second: Triggering Moments What specific situations spark your stress response? Note exact scenarios: "When my boss asks for last-minute changes" or "When my partner uses that tone of voice." Include even small triggers that you might usually ignore.

Third: Your Default Response How do you typically react? Write down your automatic behaviors: "Immediately check phone," or "Start cleaning frantically," or "Withdraw from conversation." No judgment here—just honest observation.

At week's end, look for patterns. Notice which situations consistently trigger stress, how your body signals rising tension, and your habitual ways of responding. This awareness becomes your foundation for working differently with stress.

Stress flows between your body and environment like a constant conversation, keeping you safe, alert, and responsive to life's demands. You can't eliminate this dialogue, nor should you try. Your body will always respond to pressure, your mind will always work to protect you, and these natural responses shape how you meet each moment.

As you move forward, notice how this stress response shows up in your daily life. When do you feel most alert? When does protection shift into overreaction? Take a moment now to sit quietly and observe your current state. Notice your breath, any tension in your muscles, and the quality of your thoughts. This simple act of turning attention inward opens the door to working differently with stress. In the next chapter, we'll explore how mindfulness provides practical tools to help you navigate stress with more ease and clarity.

Reflection: Take three slow breaths and notice:

Where does your body hold tension right now?

What level of alertness do you feel?

How does your mind respond to this moment of pause?

Mindfulness is how we can root ourselves to the present, to the now, this next chapter is going to teach us all that we need to know on how to keep our feet firmly planted to the ground, in the now, in our bodies.

Chapter Two

MINDFULNESS
FOR EVERYDAY CALM

Life happens in the now. In the spaces between breaths, between thoughts, between moments. Yet how often do we actually live there? We rush through breakfast thinking about work. We shower while planning our day. We listen to our children while scrolling through emails. Always somewhere else, always one step ahead or behind the actual moment we're in.

Last week, my phone died during my morning coffee ritual. No emails to check, no news to scroll through, no distractions to fill the quiet. Just me and my coffee. At first, it felt uncomfortable- this stillness, this silence. Then something shifted. I noticed the steam rising from my cup, the way the morning light painted shadows on my kitchen wall, the warmth spreading through my chest with each sip. For five minutes, I wasn't thinking about my to-do list or what happened yesterday. I was just... there.

That's what woke me up, not the coffee, but the realization of how rarely I actually taste it. How rarely do any of us taste our food, feel our feet on the ground, and listen fully to the people we love? We've become so skilled at doing many things at once that we've forgotten how to do just one thing fully.

This chapter isn't about adding another task to your day. It's about finding your way back to moments that are already waiting for you.

DEFINING TRUE MINDFULNESS

Most people hear "mindfulness" and picture someone sitting cross-legged on a mountaintop, completely removed from real life. But true mindfulness lives in ordinary moments; in morning coffee, in traffic jams, in conversations with friends. It's not about escaping your life; it's about showing up for it fully.

Science tells us something fascinating about mindfulness: When we practice being present, our brains actually change. The areas responsible for focus, memory, and emotional balance get stronger, like muscles developing through exercise. This isn't mystical—it's measurable. Brain scans show these changes clearly in people who practice regular mindfulness.

Let me show you what this looks like in real life. When someone's talking to you, mindfulness means actually listening instead of planning what you'll say next. When eating dinner, it means tasting your food instead of scrolling through your phone. When walking your dog, it means feeling the ground under your feet instead of rushing through your mental to-do list.

Think of mindfulness as training your attention muscle. Just like you might do bicep curls at the gym, you can strengthen your ability to stay present. Start with your breath—feel the air moving in and out of your body. Notice when your mind wanders (it will), and gently bring it back. This simple practice builds the foundation for staying present in more challenging moments.

Each moment offers a chance to practice. The warmth of water on your hands while washing dishes. The weight of your body as you walk to your car. The sound of your child's voice telling you about their day. These aren't interruptions to your life—they are your life, happening right now.

EVERYDAY MINDFULNESS PRACTICES

Your breath moves through you roughly 20,000 times each day, flowing through every moment whether you notice it or not. This constant companion offers a direct path to presence, transforming ordinary moments into opportunities for mindful awareness.

When you turn your attention to your breath, you create space between yourself and the constant stream of thoughts and reactions. Your breath reflects your state—shallow and quick with anxiety, slow and steady with calm. By learning to observe these patterns, you develop a natural barometer for your inner weather.

Practice Now: Feel the air moving in and out of your body. Notice where the sensation appears most clearly—nose, chest, or belly. Let your breath flow naturally for three full cycles. When your mind wanders, guide it back to the sensation of breathing. Even one minute of conscious breathing can reset your nervous system and anchor you in the present moment.

Mindful Breathing Basics

Breath is a constant companion, moving through your body roughly 20,000 times a day, whether you notice it or not. It flows through your triumphs and breakdowns, your busy moments and quiet spaces, your sleep and your waking. Most of the time, this vital force operates on autopilot-but turning your attention to it transforms breath into a powerful tool for presence.

Mindful breathing creates space between you and your thoughts, feelings, and reactions. When anxiety rises, your breath becomes shallow and quick. When relaxation deepens, your breath flows slowly and steadily. Each pattern tells you something about your current state.

Let's practice this together:

Right now, feel the air moving in and out of your body. Notice where you feel it most clearly -maybe in your nose, your chest, or your belly. Let your breath flow naturally. Notice three full cycles. Feel the natural pause between inhaling and exhaling. Observe the slight differences between each breath.

Your mind will wander to thoughts, plans, or worries. Simply guide it back to the sensation of breathing. Show yourself the same patience you'd offer a child learning something new. Each return to the breath builds your capacity for presence.

Start with short periods—even one minute of conscious breathing can reset your nervous system and bring you back to the present moment.

Eating with Awareness

If you watch any lunch break at work, you'll most likely find someone scrolling on their phone while eating, another typing with one hand and holding a sandwich with the other, someone else rushing through their meal between meetings. This constant multitasking turns eating into another task to complete rather than a moment to pause and nourish ourselves.

Mindful eating starts with a simple choice: just eat. Clear your space of everything except your food. No devices, no work, no distractions. Notice the temperature of each bite, the textures that meet your tongue, and the flavors that develop as you chew. Your body knows the natural rhythm of eating—when to take another bite, when to pause, when you've had enough.

Reflection Questions:

What changes when you give your full attention to eating?

Which sensations surprise you when you slow down?

Where does your mind try to pull you away?

How does your relationship with food shift when you eat with awareness?

Pick one meal today to practice eating with awareness. Notice what emerges when you give yourself this space to simply be present with your food.

Mindful Listening

When someone speaks, do you hear beyond their words? The tremor in their voice when nervous, their eyes lighting up with enthusiasm, the pause before sharing something meaningful? Most conversations become tennis matches where we focus on preparing our response rather than truly understanding what's being shared.

True listening demands your complete presence. Watch how someone holds their body as they talk, notice their gestures, and let their words land before forming your response. When you listen this way, people feel truly heard. Simple exchanges transform into moments of genuine connection.

Practice this first with everyday encounters with the barista taking your order, a friend sharing their day, or a colleague's quick story. Just listen. Stay present. Notice what changes.

Reflection:

Choose one conversation today to practice mindful listening. Notice:

What changed when you focused fully on the speaker?

What did you observe that you usually miss?

How did this affect the quality of your connection?

What made staying present challenging?

Technology Breaks

I love a good digital escape as much as the next person, but sometimes scrolling becomes breathing—automatic, constant, unconscious. Our phones have become extra limbs, our screens the first thing we reach for in the morning and the last thing we see at night.

Technology breaks aid in creating intentional gaps in our constant connection, so choose specific screen-free times that make sense for your life. Maybe it's the first hour after waking then let your body and mind wake up naturally instead of jumping straight into the world's demands. During the digital sunsets, notice what emerges. Is it the sound of your family moving through the house? The way evening light plays on your walls? or the thoughts and feelings that you've been too busy to notice; just allow these gaps to become spaces for presence.

MAKING IT WORK IN REAL LIFE

Life rarely happens according to plan. We can plan and make sure we're resourced enough, have our schedules organized, our intentions set. Then the baby gets sick, or work calls with an emergency, or the car breaks down. Real life has a way of interrupting our best-laid plans for peace and presence.

Most mindfulness books paint pictures of serene morning routines—meditation cushions, sunrise yoga, peaceful journaling with a steaming cup of tea. But let's talk about actual mornings: hitting snooze three times, rushing through breakfast, answering emails while brushing your teeth, and multitasking your way through chaos.

Here's the thing: mindfulness thrives in this mess. It grows stronger in the gaps between chaos, in the breath between meetings, in the pause before answering your ringing phone. You don't need to change your life to practice presence. You just need to show up differently for the life you already have. This is how you make it work, day by day moment for moment.

Finding Practice Pockets

Your day already holds natural pauses-those brief moments between activities. Each red light can become three conscious breaths. The walk to your next meeting becomes a chance to feel your feet on the ground. Standing in line at the store offers a moment to notice the sensations in your body. Washing dishes transforms into a practice of feeling water temperature, watching soap bubbles, and hearing the clink of plates.

These moments become part of your natural flow. While waiting for your coffee to brew, feel your feet on the floor. During your morning shower, notice the sensation of water on your skin. As you drive, feel your hands on the steering wheel.

Choose specific triggers-everyday moments that remind you to pay attention. Maybe it's walking through doorways, checking your phone, or hearing a particular sound. Let these regular occurrences become bells of mindfulness, calling you back to the present moment. One consistent practice, however small, creates the foundation for everything else to follow.

Dealing with Reality

I was speaking with my neighbor the other day and she told me how she'd given up on mindfulness because her house was too chaotic—three kids, two dogs, and endless interruptions. Let's talk about how to work with real life, not around it.

When the kids interrupt your morning practice, include them. Let them sit with you for one minute of belly breathing. When they get restless after ten seconds, that's fine—you've practiced presence together, however briefly.

During back-to-back meetings, take twenty seconds between calls to feel your feet on the ground, notice your breath, and reset your attention. When your mind races with deadlines during these moments, simply note "planning thoughts" and return to the sensation of breathing.

If your phone constantly demands attention, turn each notification into a reminder to pause. Before responding to that text, take one conscious breath. Before checking that email, feel your body in your chair.

MINDFUL MOMENTS PLAN

Turn everyday activities into opportunities for mindfulness. Fill in activities that fit naturally into your day, and then note how you'll bring awareness to each moment.

Morning Activities

Choose one regular morning task.

Activity (Example: Making coffee): ----------------------------

How to make it mindful: --------------------------------------

Time needed: ---

Potential challenges: --

Movement Activities

Pick a physical activity you do daily.

Activity (Example: Walking to work): -------------------------

How to make it mindful: --------------------------------------

Time needed: ---

Potential challenges: --

Work/Study Activities

Select one task you do regularly.

Activity: _____

How to make it mindful: _____

Time needed: _____

Potential challenges: _____

Evening Wind-Down

Choose one evening routine activity.

Activity: _____

How to make it mindful: _____

Time needed: _____

Potential challenges: _____

Weekly Check-In

Which moments worked best? _____

What made them effective? _____

What needs adjusting? _____

Where can you add new mindful moments? _____

Just start small. Choose moments that already exist in your day rather than trying to add new activities.

When anxiety or worry floods in during quiet moments, give it space to be there. Name it: "worry is here" or "planning mind is active." Then gently return your attention to something concrete—your breath, your footsteps, the warmth of your coffee cup.

I know, I know that it is far much easier to read about mindfulness than to practice it. Easier to plan the perfect morning routine than to work with the messy one you have. Easier to dream about quiet moments than to find presence in noisy ones, but this practice is more about choosing to show up for your life exactly as it is. Start small. Start where you are. Let each return to presence, each conscious breath, each moment of awareness be enough. Acceptance, as we'll discuss in the next chapter, will teach you that your life, in all its beautiful chaos, is happening right now. Don't wait for perfect conditions to begin.

Chapter Three
RADICAL ACCEPTANCE IN ACTION

At some point, you decide. You decide that this is where you are rooted. You make the decision to be happy, right where you are, regardless of circumstances, regardless of what life has handed you. Not because everything is perfect, but because fighting against what already is only creates more suffering.

Last week, I watched a friend struggle with a health diagnosis she couldn't change. She spent months fighting against it, researching alternatives, denying its reality, exhausting herself with "what-ifs" and "if-onlys." Then one morning, something shifted. "This is where I am," she said. "I can keep fighting it, or I can learn to live from here."

That's how radical acceptance offers a shift in how we meet our challenges. It's about acknowledging what is, exactly as it is, even when it's not what we wanted or hoped for. This isn't giving up. It's opening up to reality instead of battling it.

UNDERSTANDING RADICAL ACCEPTANCE

I didn't get the job, but that doesn't mean I'm unworthy. They ignored me after I reached out, but it still doesn't take away from who I am. The relationship ended, but that doesn't diminish my capacity to love.

Radical acceptance is meeting each moment with clear eyes and an open heart. When your partner says they need space, you can acknowledge their need while honoring your own feelings. When illness changes your daily routine, you can adapt to new limitations while still pursuing what matters to you. When loss visits, you can feel its full weight while knowing your capacity to carry it.

it is essentially standing firmly in your truth while facing life's storms. The rain falls, and you see it simply as rain; not punishment, not personal failure, just water falling from clouds. The wind blows, and you feel it as wind-not the universe conspiring against you, just air moving through space. You see each moment exactly as it appears, free from the weight of judgment or blame.

This kind of acceptance requires both strength and softness; the strength to stay present with difficult truths, and the softness to hold them with compassion. You can feel pain without making it mean something about your worth. You can face challenges without turning them into stories about deserving or not deserving.

This isn't resignation because resignation collapses in defeat. Acceptance stands in strength, saying "This is where I am, and from here I can move forward."

Common Misconceptions

I think that it is normal to want to fight against acceptance. Our minds tell us stories about what acceptance means, and these stories often keep us stuck. Here are the most common misconceptions I've encountered in my work:

❑ **Accepting means approving:** Acceptance simply means acknowledging what exists right now. You can accept a difficult situation while still believing it should be different. Like accepting rain while wishing for sunshine-acknowledging the weather doesn't mean you prefer it.

❑ **Acceptance equals giving up:** Actually, acceptance creates the foundation for change. You must first know where you stand to move forward effectively. Just as you need to know your current location to plot a new course.

❑ **Acceptance makes you passive:** You can accept your current reality while taking active steps to change it. Acceptance focuses on seeing clearly, not determining your response. You might accept feeling anxious before a presentation while still choosing to speak.

THE COST OF NON-ACCEPTANCE

When you fight against reality, your body pays the price. what I mean is that your muscles stay tense, ready for battle. Your breath becomes shallow, preparing for the next hit. Your digestion suffers, your immune system weakens, and your energy depletes. The constant state of resistance keeps your stress response activated, wearing down your physical resources.

Emotionally, it also creates layers of suffering. There's the original pain-the loss, the change, the disappointment. Then there's the suffering you add by fighting it. The "this shouldn't be happening" thoughts. The "I can't handle this" beliefs. The endless replay of how things should have been different.

This creates a cycle: The more you resist, the more tension you carry. The more tension you carry, the harder it becomes to see clearly. The harder it becomes to see clearly, the more you struggle. Each round of resistance adds another layer of suffering to the original difficulty.

WHEN ACCEPTANCE FEELS IMPOSSIBLE

My first pet passed away when I was twelve. I spent weeks refusing to walk past her favorite spots in the house, avoiding her empty bed, denying the reality of her absence. The pain felt too big to hold, too heavy to accept. Sometimes life hands us moments that feel impossible to embrace, but it doesn't mean that you can't leave any room open. There's more than enough space, and you, in all your humanness have more than enough capacity.

Working Through Trauma

Trauma changes how your brain and body process reality. Your muscles might stay tense even in safe places. Your mind might race with memories when you try to rest. Your nervous system might read danger in ordinary moments. This makes acceptance feel like an impossible task.

Here's what helps: Start with accepting where you are right now. If you can't sleep through the night, accept that this is your current reality. If certain places or people trigger difficult memories, accept that your body is trying to protect you. If some days feel harder than others, accept that healing moves at its own pace.

This kind of acceptance creates space for healing. When you stop fighting against your responses, when you stop blaming yourself for not being "over it," your body begins to trust that it's safe to heal. You might notice small changes—moments of peace between the hard times, brief periods when your body relaxes, and gradual shifts in how you respond to triggers.

Meeting Grief

I have been alive long enough to know that grief writes its own rules. One day you're fine, handling everything with surprising strength. The next day, the sight of their coffee mug in the cupboard brings you to your knees. There's no timeline, no proper way to carry the loss.

And it's not just the loss of loved ones we grieve. Sometimes, it's the person we thought we'd become by now-that confident self who would have it all figured out. Sometimes it's the dreams we held so carefully—the career that didn't unfold, the relationship that never blossomed, the life we imagined that took a different turn. Sometimes we grieve versions of ourselves we had to leave behind.

Here's what helps: Write letters to the life you thought you'd have. Speak to the version of yourself you had to let go. Create rituals for the invisible losses- light a candle for the career path you didn't take, plant something for the relationship that ended, and take a quiet moment to honor the dreams that changed shape.

Each time grief surfaces, give it space to breathe; if memories of an old friendship hit during your morning coffee, allow yourself to remember without any guilt, judgement, or shame. If regret about a choice arises during your commute, acknowledge it. If sadness about a lost dream appears before sleep, hold it gently. However brief these moments of acceptance are, they will help your heart process what it needs to release.

Facing Injustice

Part of what it means to be human is that you will wrong people and be wronged. You will face situations that feel deeply unfair. You will witness injustice that makes your blood boil and your heartache. These moments test the very limits of acceptance.

Accepting injustice doesn't mean approving of what happened. It means acknowledging the reality clearly enough to take effective action. When someone dismisses your work because of your gender, acceptance means seeing this bias for what it is. When systems discriminate, acceptance means recognizing the real barriers you face.

This kind of acceptance fuels change rather than defeat. It means channeling your anger into advocacy rather than letting it burn you up inside. It means using your pain to connect with others facing similar struggles. It means transforming your experience into wisdom that can help create change.

Start by accepting where things stand right now. See the situation without minimizing or exaggerating. Feel your natural responses: the anger, the hurt, the desire for justice. Let these feelings inform your actions without letting them control your choices. This balance between accepting what is and working for what should be creates the foundation for meaningful change.

HOW TO PRACTICE ACCEPTANCE

If you take each day to tell yourself that growth happens in small steps, not giant leaps, you begin to understand how acceptance becomes a practice. Let me show you how to build this practice in real, tangible ways.

❑ **Learn to notice your resistance:** Start by paying attention to when you tighten against life. Notice the physical signs first: a clenched jaw, tight shoulders, shallow breathing. These body signals usually appear before your mind catches up. When someone criticizes your work, feel how your body responds before your thoughts start defending. When plans change unexpectedly, notice your first physical reaction.

❑ **Question your patterns:** Look closely at your automatic responses to difficulty. When things go wrong, do you immediately jump to blame? Do you retreat into busyness? Do you try to control everything around you? Write down your common reactions. Each pattern shows you where acceptance needs to grow.

❑ **Nurture your inner child:** That part of you that resists most strongly often comes from old wounds, from times when acceptance felt dangerous. Speak to this part of yourself with compassion. When resistance rises, acknowledge the fear beneath it. "I understand you're trying to protect me. We're safe enough to look at this now."

❏ **Practice daily:** Start with small situations-traffic jams, minor inconveniences, and slight disappointments. These become your training ground. Feel the initial resistance. Notice the urge to fight reality. Then consciously choose to soften, to open, to accept what is. Let these small moments build your capacity for accepting bigger challenges.

Just This Moment Exercise

When life presents a challenge, we often rush to fix, change, or escape it. This exercise helps you practice pausing and accepting what's here right now, even if just for a moment. Choose a current situation that brings up resistance-nothing too overwhelming, but something that regularly creates tension in your life.

Take a quiet moment now. Think of your chosen situation. Notice the physical sensations that arise. Where does your body hold tension? What thoughts surface? Instead of trying to change anything, simply say to yourself: "Just for this moment, can I accept that this is happening?" Stay with whatever emerges-sensations, thoughts, feelings. Notice what shifts when you open to acceptance, even briefly.

Write your observations here:

EXPLORING YOUR RESISTANCE: A WORKSHEET

Notice where you resist reality most strongly. Pick situations that repeatedly create tension in your life, then explore how acceptance might shift your experience.

Area of Resistance

Situation: _____

How I typically react: _____

What I try to control: _____

Cost of this resistance: _____

Moving Toward Acceptance

What I'm afraid will happen if I accept this: _____

_____

What's actually true right now: _____

_____

What might change if I stopped fighting reality: _____

_____

Finding New Responses

One small step toward acceptance: _____

What support I need: _____

What I might learn: _____

Choose three situations to work with:

Daily Friction

(Example: Morning traffic)

Current response: _____

Possible shift: _____

Relationship Challenge

Current response: _____

Possible shift: _____

Personal Struggle

Current response: _____

Possible shift: _____

What patterns do you notice?

_____

_____

Which area feels most important to work with?

_____

_____

What's your first step?

_____

I can spend all day telling you that acceptance is the path to peace, that fighting reality only creates more suffering, and that letting go will set you free. But acceptance isn't something you can be talked into. It's a practice you choose, moment by moment, breath by breath. Sometimes it looks like facing a hard truth about yourself. Sometimes it means sitting with uncomfortable feelings. Sometimes it means acknowledging that life isn't going according to plan. But always, acceptance offers the same gift: the freedom to start from where you actually are, not where you wish you were. This is where real change begins. Let's go and unpack the concept of emotional clarity.

Chapter Four

EMOTIONAL CLARITY WITH ACT TOOLS

We struggle so much with big feelings because the focus has always been to get rid of them, instead of learning to sit with and learn from them. Think about how we talk about emotions: "Stop crying." "Don't be angry." "Just calm down." As if feelings were problems to solve rather than experiences to understand.

From an early age, we learn to push away difficult emotions. Sadness gets buried under busyness. Anger gets swallowed with "I'm fine." Anxiety gets masked with control. We become experts at avoiding what we feel, but terrible at understanding it.

This chapter offers a different approach. Instead of fighting your emotions or trying to change them, you'll learn to read them like messages from your inner world. You'll discover how naming your feelings can actually reduce their grip. You'll explore practical tools for working with difficult thoughts and emotions, not to make them go away, but to understand what they're trying to tell you.

When you learn to meet your emotions with clarity instead of resistance, something shifts. The feelings don't necessarily change, but your relationship with them does. And that makes all the difference.

UNDERSTANDING EMOTIONAL LITERACY

The human emotional system operates with remarkable complexity, but Most people use only a handful of words to describe their emotional states; that's primarily "good," "bad," "fine," or "okay." This limited emotional vocabulary creates a barrier to understanding and working with our internal experiences.

Primary emotions are direct responses to situations, especially the immediate fear when facing danger, the natural sadness of loss, and the quick spark of anger at injustice. These emotions serve essential functions in human survival and social connection. Secondary emotions, however, develop as reactions to our primary emotions, like feeling ashamed about being afraid, getting angry about feeling sad, and becoming anxious about being angry.

Common blind spots become more evident in our emotional awareness. Many people mistake bodily sensations for emotions, failing to distinguish between feeling "tired" and feeling "discouraged," or between feeling "tense" and feeling "anxious." Others struggle to identify emotions until they reach extreme intensity, missing early warning signs that could help them respond more effectively.

Building emotional vocabulary requires systematic observation and clear distinctions. Start by learning to identify basic emotional families: anger, fear, sadness, joy, disgust, and surprise. Within each family exist subtle variations. Anger, for instance, ranges from mild irritation to full rage, each variation carrying different intensities and action tendencies.

THE "NAME IT TO TAME IT" TECHNIQUE

When you name an emotion accurately, your brain begins a powerful shift. The simple act of labeling feelings like "This is anxiety" or "I notice frustration" calms your brain's alarm center while activating areas that help you think clearly. This biological response explains why putting feelings into words helps you feel more balanced.

Think of this like turning on a light in a dark room. Before naming the emotion, you might feel overwhelmed by unclear sensations and reactions. But when you label what you feel, the landscape becomes clearer, making emotions easier to understand and manage. This skill grows stronger with practice, helping you navigate emotional states with more confidence and clarity.

This process works in simple measurable steps:

Step One: Physical Awareness

Start with your body's signals. Map the physical sensations:

❑ Where in your body do you feel the emotion?

❑ What's the quality of the sensation-tight, hot, heavy, hollow?

❑ How intense is it on a scale of 1-10?

❑ Is it moving or static?

❑ What's its shape or size?

Step Two: Emotional Tone

Before naming specific emotions, identify the broader category:

❑ Is this feeling drawing you in or pushing you away?

❑ Does it make you want to move or freeze?

❑ Is it energizing or depleting?

❑ Does it feel familiar or new?

Step Three: Specific Naming

Move from general to specific labels:

- ❑ Instead of "bad," Ask if you are frustrated? Disappointed? Hurt?
- ❑ Instead of "good". Are you content? Excited? Peaceful?
- ❑ Instead of "stressed". Are you overwhelmed? Pressured? Anxious?

Step Four: Emotional Layering

Look for emotions that might be hiding under the obvious ones:

- ❑ Under anger, you might find fear
- ❑ Under irritability, you might find exhaustion
- ❑ Under anxiety, you might find excitement
- ❑ Notice which emotions commonly pair together for you

This systematic approach allows you to build emotional clarity over time, leading to more effective regulation.

Common Challenges

Many of us learned to handle emotions in ways that seemed helpful but actually blocked us from deeper understanding. Through years of clinical practice and research, we've identified several key patterns that prevent effective emotional awareness. Let's examine three common challenges and explore practical solutions for each:

Wanting to fix too quickly

Many of us rush to fix emotions before fully understanding them, but that is like putting on a bandaid on a wound you haven't cleaned, labeling too quickly can cover up what needs attention. When anxiety hits, you might quickly label it "stress about work" without noticing it's actually fear of failure, or loneliness, or a need for validation.

The Solution: Give yourself sixty seconds to just feel before naming. Notice the physical sensation. Let it be there without rushing to label or fix it. Only then, start the naming process.

Analysing too much

Some people get stuck in their heads, treating emotions like puzzles to solve. They spend hours analyzing "why" they feel something instead of experiencing the feeling itself. This intellectual approach creates distance from the actual emotion, making it harder to work with effectively.

The Solution: When you catch yourself analyzing, bring your attention back to your body. What sensations tell you this emotion is present? Where do you feel it physically? Let the direct experience guide your understanding.

Vaguely labeling.

Using broad terms like "stressed," "fine," or "upset" keeps you from truly understanding your emotional landscape. These umbrella terms can hide more specific emotions that need attention.

The Solution: Challenge yourself to add one more specific word. Instead of just "stressed," ask "What kind of stress?" Instead of "fine," ask "What does fine feel like right now?"

DEFUSION TOOLS FOR DAILY LIFE

Your mind produces thousands of thoughts daily. "I'm not good enough." "This will go wrong." "I can't handle this." Often, we believe these thoughts as if they're undeniable facts rather than seeing them as what they are just thoughts. Defusion tools help you step back and see thoughts as mental events rather than absolute truths. "Leaves on a Stream" Practice.

Close your eyes. Picture a gentle stream with leaves floating past. As thoughts arise, place each one on a leaf. Watch it drift away. Don't try to push thoughts away or hold onto them. Simply notice "Having the thought..." and let it float on by. Practice this for five minutes daily, especially when thoughts feel overwhelming. Here are some of the most useful ones.

"Thank You, Mind" Technique

This acknowledges your mind's protective instincts. The idea behind this is that your mind evolved to scan for danger, to anticipate problems, and to keep you safe. When it tells you, "You can't handle this," before a big presentation, it's trying to protect you from potential social threats. When it whispers "Don't try" before a new challenge, it wants to save you from possible failure.

Here's how to practice it: When a difficult thought arises, name it clearly: "I'm having the thought that I'll fail." Then respond with acknowledgment: "Thank you, mind, for trying to protect me." Notice how this feels different from arguing with the thought or trying to push it away.

Try this in everyday situations:

❏ When anxious about a deadline: "Thank you, mind, for caring about doing good work."

❑ When worried about a relationship: "Thank you, mind, for wanting to keep me safe from hurt."

❑ When doubting a decision: "Thank you, mind, for trying to help me make good choices."

Ultimately you want to change your relationships with your negative thoughts. Your mind will keep doing its job of generating protective thoughts. You can acknowledge this while choosing how to respond to them.

The Observer Exercise

Your mind is constantly producing thoughts, like a radio playing in the background, it sometimes broadcasts worries, sometimes memories, sometimes plans for the future. The following exercise teaches you to recognize yourself as the one who is listening to the radio rather than being the broadcast itself.

Here's the practice:

Sit quietly for a moment. Notice a thought that's present right now. Take a small step back and say: "I'm noticing I'm having the thought..." For example, with the thought "I'm not prepared," say "I'm noticing I'm having the thought that I'm not prepared."

This creates three clear parts:

❑ You-the one observing

❑ The act of noticing

❑ The thought itself

Practice with different thoughts throughout your day:

❑ With self-talk: "I'm noticing the thought that I'm not good enough"

❑ With worries: "I'm noticing the thought that things will go wrong"

❑ With memories: "I'm noticing the thought about that embarrassing moment"

You are the sky that is holding all sorts of weather patterns that pass through. You remain the constant observer while thoughts, like clouds, move through your awareness. This practice builds your capacity to hold any thought while maintaining your sense of self as something larger than any single thought.

Working with Difficult

Before every important meeting, your mind might tell you "You'll mess this up." During social events, it might whisper "Everyone thinks you're awkward." While parenting, thoughts like "You're not doing enough" might surface repeatedly. These thoughts stick around, playing on repeat despite your best efforts to silence them.

Start by tracking these persistent thoughts in specific situations:

❑ During work meetings

❑ Before social events

❑ When making important decisions

❑ In quiet moments alone

Pay attention to their timing and triggers:

❑ Does self-doubt appear before every team presentation?

❑ Do you worry about health spikes when you're overtired?

❑ Does criticism of others surface when you feel insecure?

Then experiment with carrying these thoughts differently:

❏ When self-criticism shows up before a presentation, try saying "Here's my old friend, the 'not good enough' thought"

❏ When worry appears about your children, notice "My mind is doing its job of trying to protect them"

❏ When perfectionism rises, observe "I'm having the 'everything must be perfect' thought again"

The goal becomes working with these thoughts rather than trying to eliminate them. Like learning to walk in the rain without fighting each raindrop, you can learn to move forward with difficult thoughts without letting them control your actions.

WHEN EMOTIONS FEEL TOO BIG

Sometimes, things feel a little too big; like tidal waves crashing all over you, leaving you gasping for air, struggling to find solid ground. Those moments when anxiety floods your chest, when grief knocks you sideways, when anger burns so hot you can barely think straight.

Immediate Stabilization

Focus first on basic safety; allow yourself to feel your feet on the floor. Notice five things that you can see, then take three deep breaths that make your belly rise. Run cold water over your wrists. These simple physical actions help your nervous system begin to settle.

Creating Space

When emotions feel overwhelming, your first instinct might be to contract, to make yourself smaller, to try to contain what feels uncontainable. Instead, give the emotion room to move. Start by naming it specifically: "This is overwhelming grief" or "This is intense fear." This naming creates initial breathing room between you and the emotion.

Then create literal, physical space. Step outside where the sky can hold some of what feels too big for you. Move to a different room, breaking the emotional loop that can build in one spot. Stand up if you've been sitting, or sit down if you've been pacing. Change your physical position in any way that feels accessible right now.

Even small changes in location can shift emotional intensity. Moving from your desk to the window, from the couch to the kitchen, from inside to your front step-each change gives your nervous system a chance to reset. Your body begins to register that while the emotion might feel permanent, you can still move, still choose, and still take active steps.

This practice, both through naming and moving, reminds you that you're larger than any single emotion. You're the container for these feelings, not the feelings themselves.

Building Capacity

The resources that sustain us are the things that usually build up slowly, and steadily, over time. Like muscles strengthening through regular use, or roots growing deeper with each storm they weather. Your capacity to handle big emotions grows the same way; through meeting them again and again.

Building emotional capacity happens in layers: First, through recognition, learning to spot the early signals before emotions become overwhelming. The slight tension in your shoulders that precedes anxiety. The heaviness in your chest that comes before sadness. These physical cues become your early warning system.

Then through experience, each time you move through intense emotion, you learn something valuable. What helped you stay grounded? Which tools worked best? Keep track of these lessons. They become your personal map for navigating future emotional storms.

Finally, through trust, trust in your ability to handle whatever comes up. You'll handle it because you've handled difficult emotions before. Each wave of feeling that you survive, each moment of intensity that passes, builds evidence that you can move through hard feelings and emerge on the other side.

Leaves on a Stream: A Visualization Exercise

Imagine a gentle stream flowing past you, carrying leaves that drift by on the water's surface. Each leaf can hold a thought that occupies your mind. This practice helps you observe your thoughts without getting caught in them.

Your Stream Visualization

First, notice your recurring thoughts:

Write down thoughts that show up often:

Circle the ones that tend to hook you most:

Now, place each thought on a leaf:

Thought:

_____

_____

Watch it float by: How does it feel to let it drift?

_____

_____

What happens as it moves downstream?

_____

_____

Continue with more thoughts:

Thought:

_____

_____

As it drifts:

_____

_____

What changes?:

_____

_____

_____

Notice which thoughts:

Try to make you grab them: _____

Feel harder to let go: _____

Float away easily: _____

Remember: The goal isn't to clear your mind but to practice watching thoughts pass like leaves on water. Some thoughts will catch your attention more than others. Simply notice this and return to watching the stream flow.

What did you discover about your thoughts?

_____

_____

Habits only stick if you commit to showing up consistently, let me go and show you how you can make your mindfulness practice more sustainable.

Chapter Five

SUSTAINING MINDFULNESS PRACTICES

The gap between knowing and doing is a lot wider than we'd like to admit. You might understand the benefits of mindfulness perfectly well. You might even have experienced its power firsthand, but turning that knowledge into daily practice is where the real work begins.

Most of us have experienced moments of clarity, of deep presence, of genuine peace. Maybe it happened during a quiet morning walk, in the middle of an engaging conversation, or even during a crisis when everything suddenly became crystal clear. These moments show us what's possible. But they also highlight the challenge: how do we build a bridge between these occasional experiences and our daily lives?

The answer lies not in dramatic changes or perfect practices, but in understanding how habits actually form. Real change happens in small moments, repeated consistently. It grows through daily choices that might seem insignificant on their own but accumulate into lasting transformation.

This teaches you how to build that bridge; how to take mindfulness from a nice idea or occasional practice and weave it into the fabric of your daily life. Not through force or rigid rules, but through understanding how lasting habits actually form.

THE SCIENCE BEHIND HABIT FORMATION

If you speak to the majority of people on January first, they will tell you they're ready to transform their lives. New gym memberships surge, meditation apps get downloaded, and plans get made. By February, most of these commitments have faded. This pattern reveals something crucial about how habits actually work; and why most attempts at forming them fail.

Your brain forms habits through a clear sequence: trigger, behavior, and reward. Each time this sequence repeats, neural pathways strengthen. But here's what most people miss: these pathways build gradually, through consistent repetition, not through intensity or willpower.

The science shows that successful habit formation depends less on motivation and more on design. Small, consistent actions repeated in stable contexts create stronger habits than ambitious plans without clear triggers. Your brain responds better to "After I pour my morning coffee, I'll take three mindful breaths" than to "I'll meditate for an hour every day."

Common misconceptions about habits lead people astray:

❑ Believing motivation must come first

❑ Expecting too much too soon

❑ Relying on willpower alone

❑ Starting with practices too big to sustain

❑ Looking for perfect conditions

Understanding how your brain actually builds habits lets you work with your natural tendencies rather than against them. Let's explore how to apply this knowledge to building lasting mindfulness practices.

HABIT STACKING FUNDAMENTALS

Habit formation is simple biology: your brain likes to conserve energy by automating regular behaviors. Just like you don't think about how to tie your shoes or brush your teeth anymore, you can build mindfulness into your daily routines until it becomes just as automatic.

Habit stacking uses this natural tendency by linking new practices to existing habits. Instead of trying to create entirely new routines, you attach mindfulness practices to things you already do consistently. Your morning coffee becomes a cue for three mindful breaths. Stopping at red lights signals a moment to check in with your body. Walking through doorways reminds you to notice your surroundings.

Choose anchor points that:

❑ Happens reliably every day

❑ Have a clear beginning and end

❑ Occur in relatively stable conditions

❑ Already have your full attention

For example:

❑ The moment between turning off your car and entering work

❑ The first sip of your morning drink

❑ The transition between ending work and heading home

❑ The pause before picking up your phone.

The key lies in choosing one small practice and one reliable trigger. Master that single combination first. Maybe it's three breaths before your morning coffee. Practice this one connection until it feels natural, then build from there. Small steps, taken consistently, create lasting change.

MINDFUL MOMENTS MAP

Match each mindful practice with a daily trigger that fits naturally:

Quick Practices (1-3 breaths):

Practice: _____

Daily Trigger: _____

Time of Day: _____

Body Check-ins:

Practice: _____

Daily Trigger: _____

Time of Day: _____

Present Moment Awareness:

Practice: _____

Daily Trigger: _____

Time of Day: _____

Reviewing Your Map:

Easiest connection to make: _____

Most challenging link: _____

When you'll need reminders: _____

Success Strategies:

Visual cue you'll use:_____

How you'll handle missed practices:_____

_____

_____

What support you need: _____

_____

_____

Start Date: _____ Review Date: _____

This week I commit to: _____

_____

_____

Blueprint Exercise: Creating Your Practice

Life moves in natural rhythms. Your energy rises and falls throughout the day. Your mind feels clear at certain hours and foggy at others. Some moments naturally invite presence while others scatter your attention. Building a sustainable mindfulness practice means working with these rhythms, not against them.

This exercise helps you map your natural patterns and find the right moments to integrate mindfulness practices. Think of it as creating a personalized blueprint-one that matches your actual life, not some ideal version of it.

YOUR DAILY TIMELINE

Morning Hours (Wake-up to Noon)

Time: _____

Energy Level: ☐ High   ☐ Medium   ☐ Low

Regular Activities: _____

_____

Possible Practice Spot: _____

Midday Hours (Noon to 5 pm)

Time: _____

Energy Level: ☐ High   ☐ Medium   ☐ Low

Regular Activities: _____

_____

Possible Practice Spot: _____

Evening Hours (5 pm to Bedtime)

Time: _____

Energy Level: ☐ High   ☐ Medium   ☐ Low

Regular Activities: _____

_____

Possible Practice Spot: _____

Anchor Points

Circle your most consistent daily activities:

Morning Activities: _____

Regular Breaks: _____

Travel Times: _____

Meals: _____

Evening Routine: _____

Choose Your Starting Point

Select one anchor point: _____

Simple practice to add: _____

Time needed: _____

Potential obstacles: _____

Remember: Start with one small change that fits naturally into your existing routine.

Track Your Progress Here:

Day 1: _____

Day 2: _____

Day 3: _____

Notes on what worked: _____

_____

The whole purpose of this is to help you find natural places in your day where mindfulness can take root and grow, so be easy on yourself and allow yourself to show up as authentically as you can.

MANAGING TIME CONSTRAINTS

Most of us say we lack time for mindfulness while scrolling social media or replaying conversations in our heads. The time exists, we just need to use it differently. Let's explore how to work with the time you actually have, not the time you wish for.

Your day naturally contains small gaps–the pause after sending an email, the moment before entering a meeting, the breath before answering a call. These windows, often lasting just seconds, offer chances for presence. Let daily activities become practice triggers: doorways signal to feel your feet, computer startup time prompts a posture check, and red lights invite three conscious breaths.

One moment of complete presence can shift your entire day. Focus on these quality moments, tasting that first sip of coffee, feeling the water temperature during handwashing, noticing your body's weight in your chair. By weaving mindfulness into existing activities rather than seeing it as another task, practice becomes part of your natural rhythm. Let me show you how you can do that with this exercise below:

Exercise: Building Your Strategic Integration Practice

It is said that every time you check your phone, you press it around 2,617 times per day. That's 2,617 potential moments for mindfulness practice. Your daily routines contain dozens of these repeated actions–checking email, opening doors, starting your car, sipping drinks. Let's turn these automatic moments into opportunities for presence.

Take ten minutes to map out where mindfulness can naturally fit into your existing routine. You'll need:

❑ A notebook

❑ Your typical daily schedule

❑ An honest look at your regular activities

Step One: List Your Daily Constants

Write down activities that happen reliably every day:

❑ Regular meetings

❑ Commute times

❑ Meal breaks

❑ Tasks you repeat daily

Step Two: Identify Natural Pauses

For each activity, find existing transition points:

❑ Before and after meetings

❑ Between tasks

❑ During brief waits

❑ Regular breaks

Step Three: Match Mindful Moments

Choose simple practices that fit each pause:

❑ Three breaths before meetings

❑ Body awareness during elevator rides

❑ Sensory awareness during coffee breaks

❑ Posture checks while sitting

Step Four: Start With Three

Select three integration points that feel most doable. Practice these for one week before adding more. Track what works and what needs adjustment.

Remember: Success comes from choosing points where mindfulness enhances rather than disrupts your day. Start small, build gradually, and let your practice grow naturally with your routine.

Daily Log (Optional): Note which integration points worked best each day. What made them successful? What challenges arose? Use this information to refine your practice.

Let me create a different kind of template that focuses on finding and using "time pockets" for mindfulness:

TIME POCKET TRACKER

The space between finishing your shower and getting dressed. That moment when your computer starts up. The pause before you open your car door offers perfect opportunities for brief mindful moments. This tracker helps you spot these natural pauses in your day and turn them into opportunities for presence. Instead of reaching for your phone or rushing to the next task, you'll learn to use these moments differently. Think of it as creating tiny islands of calm in your busy schedule.

Morning Time Pockets

Identify 3 brief pauses in your morning:

Between: ---------------------- and --------------------------

What you usually do: _____

Mindful moment to add: _____

Between: ---------------------- and ----------------------------

What you usually do:_____

Mindful moment to add:_____

Between: ---------------------- and ----------------------------

What you usually do:_____

Mindful moment to add:_____

Work/Day Time Pockets

Spot 3 natural breaks in your workflow:

Activity pause:_____

Duration:_____

How to use it:_____

Activity pause:_____

Duration:_____

How to use it:_____

Activity pause: _____

Duration: _____

How to use it: _____

Evening Wind-Down Pockets

Find 3 transition moments:

Between: _____ and _____

Current habit: _____

New mindful use: _____

Between: _____ and _____

Current habit: _____

New mindful use: _____

Between: _____ and _____

Current habit: _____

New mindful use: _____

My Priority Pockets

Most promising time pocket: _____

Easiest to implement: _____

Most needed during my day: _____

This week I'll focus on using: _____

_____

_____

_____

I have been trying to think of a word that sums up how mindfulness becomes part of your story. When it stops being another self-help project and starts feeling like coming home to yourself. The word that keeps returning, soft as the morning light, is 'integration.'

You see it in those quiet moments—when your hand wraps around a warm coffee mug and for once, just for a breath, you're not rushing ahead to the next thing. When you're driving, and notice how your hands rest on the steering wheel, how the sun plays through your windshield. When you catch yourself actually tasting your food instead of eating while scrolling.

These moments aren't dramatic. They won't make headlines or change the world. But they change your world, one small return to presence at a time. Because mindfulness isn't about perfection or achievement. It's about remembering to come back, again and again, to this moment, to this breath, to this life that's already happening.

Conclusion

I have been trying to think of a word that sums up how mindfulness weaves into your daily life. When it stops being another task and starts feeling like coming home to yourself, that word might be 'integration.'

Integration shows up in ordinary moments; your hand wrapping around a warm coffee mug, your breath steadying before a difficult conversation, your attention fully resting on one small task. These moments of presence might seem simple, but they create a foundation for moving through life with more awareness and ease.

Take a moment now to choose your first integration point—one small action you'll pair with mindfulness. Write it down. Notice how it feels to start exactly where you are, with what you have, in this moment. Your practice begins here.

Book Three

ACT FOR OVERTHINKING AND OCD

Practical Tools to Break Free
from Intrusive Thoughts
and Reclaim Mental Clarity

Introduction

The clock reads 10:47 pm and you stand in your kitchen, staring at the stove, even though you know you turned it off before starting your bedtime routine. "I definitely switched it off," you whisper, but your mind floods with what-ifs. One more check won't hurt. Just to be sure. Just to feel safe. Three checks later, you're still there, caught between knowing and doubting, between logic and that nagging urge to check again.

Sound familiar? We all get caught in mental loops-replaying conversations, imagining worst-case scenarios, and questioning decisions we've already made. Sometimes these thought patterns grow stronger, taking up more space in our lives. Whether it's overthinking that keeps you awake at night or OCD patterns that demand your attention, these mental loops can feel impossible to escape.

Take a moment now to think about your own patterns. When does your mind tend to get stuck? What thoughts keep pulling you back for another look? What mental loops feel hardest to step out of?

This book offers a different way forward. Instead of fighting with your thoughts or trying to perfect them, you'll learn practical tools from Acceptance and Commitment Therapy (ACT) that help you relate to your mind differently. Through simple, proven techniques like defusion and acceptance, you'll discover how to create space around difficult thoughts and move forward even when your mind gets noisy.

Chapter One

THE OVERTHINKING MIND

You can spend your whole life trying to outrun your thoughts, but they'll always catch up. Your mind does what it does; it thinks, analyzes, questions, and doubts. For some of us, this natural tendency kicks into overdrive. We don't just think about things; we think about them from every angle, until thinking itself becomes exhausting.

Think of it like being stuck in a maze where every turn leads to another question, another doubt, another "what if." The exit seems close, but each step toward it opens three new pathways to explore. Let's look at how these mental mazes form, and more importantly, how to find your way through them.

HOW THOUGHT LOOPS DEVELOP

The brain processes thousands of thoughts daily, most flowing like traffic—some slow, some fast, some catching attention before moving on. But certain thoughts get stuck in circulation, playing on repeat when your mind flags them as especially important or threatening. Instead of letting these thoughts pass, you focus on them, trying to solve or prevent imagined problems. This extra attention makes the thought seem more significant, triggering your brain's threat response.

This pattern becomes more intense with OCD, following a distinct structure where intrusive thoughts create immediate distress, leading to actions meant to reduce anxiety. Think about checking a locked door. Your mind whispers, "What if it's not really locked?" This thought creates immediate tension, and checking brings brief relief. But relief fades quickly, making the urge to check again even stronger. The more you respond to these thoughts with compulsive actions, the more power they gain.

Both overthinking and OCD share this self-reinforcing nature. Your logical mind might know the door is locked or the stove is off, yet something deeper pushes you to check again, to think it through one more time, to seek absolute certainty. This explains why simple solutions fall short-you need tools that work with how your brain actually functions, addressing both the thoughts themselves and the patterns that keep them spinning.

Obsessions vs. Compulsions

Obsessions arrive uninvited in your mind. They show up as thoughts, images, or urges that feel impossible to ignore. A parent might have sudden thoughts of harming their child, even though they would never act on it. A student might fixate on the thought that they wrote something offensive in their essay, despite checking it multiple times. These thoughts create intense distress because they contradict who you are and what you value.

Compulsions emerge as responses to these obsessions. They appear logical at first—check the stove to prevent fire, wash hands to avoid illness, and arrange items perfectly to prevent harm to loved ones. But compulsions follow their own rules. One check becomes two, becomes ten. A quick handwash extends to thirty minutes of scrubbing. What starts as straightforward safety measures grows into elaborate rituals.

The relationship between obsessions and compulsions creates a self-reinforcing cycle. When you perform a compulsion, it temporarily reduces anxiety. This relief teaches your brain that the compulsion "worked," making you more likely to use it again when the obsessive thought returns. Over time, compulsions require more repetition or elaboration to provide the same relief, while obsessions grow stronger and more frequent.

This pattern differs from regular worry or perfectionism. While many people double-check important things or prefer order, OCD turns these normal behaviors into rigid requirements, attaching severe distress to any deviation from exact performance.

Mapping Your OCD Patterns: A Worksheet

When thoughts loop and urge to check, clean, or arrange to feel overwhelming, it helps to see these patterns clearly on paper. This mapping exercise guides you through each part of your OCD cycle, revealing how thoughts connect to actions and how relief becomes part of the pattern.

Identifying Your Obsessions

Obsessive thoughts often feel intense and demanding. They might show up as worries about harm, contamination, or things being "just right." In this section, notice which thoughts grip you most strongly and how they affect your body and emotions:

Common thought that appears:

When it first started: _____

What triggers it most often: _____

Physical sensations it brings: _____

Emotions it stirs up: _____

Understanding Your Compulsions

Compulsions emerge as ways to handle obsessive thoughts. They might feel like the only option in the moment, promising relief if you just check one more time or clean a little longer. Track how these actions play out:

First urge that arises:_____

Actions you take: _____

_____

How many times/how long:_____

What you believe might happen if you don't act: _____

_____

How this impacts your daily life: _____

_____

_____

The Relief Cycle

Relief plays a powerful role in maintaining OCD patterns. While compulsions might bring temporary calm, this relief often leads to stronger urges later. Map out how this cycle works for you:

Feeling right after the compulsion: _____

How long relief lasts: _____

What thoughts come next:_____

Energy this cycle takes: _____

Cost to your life: _____

Pattern Recognition

Understanding when and how your OCD intensifies helps you prepare and respond more effectively. Notice the rhythms of your symptoms:

When symptoms are strongest: _____

Times they ease up: _____

What tends to make things worse: _____.

What brings even slight relief: _____.

Reflection Questions

Take time to consider what this mapping reveals:

What surprised you about these patterns?

_____

_____

Where do you see opportunities for change?

_____

_____

What support might help?

_____

_____

One small step you could take:

_____

_____

Remember: This mapping isn't about fixing everything at once. It's about seeing your patterns clearly so you can begin working with them differently. Take your time with each section, adding notes as you notice more about how OCD moves through your life.

Common Misconceptions

If you ask most people what OCD is, they will tell you it's about being extremely clean, perfectly organized, or intensely focused on details. They might say someone is "so OCD" about color-coding their closet or keeping their desk tidy. These misconceptions minimize what OCD actually means for those who live with it.

Here are the most common ones that most people gravitate toward:

❑ **Liking Things Clean and Organized:** People believe OCD means having an immaculate home or being extremely organized. The reality involves distressing thoughts that make someone feel compelled to clean or organize to prevent imagined catastrophes. Someone might spend hours cleaning not because they enjoy cleanliness, but because their mind tells them their family will get sick and die if they stop.

❑ **Perfectionism and Attention to Detail:** While many view OCD as perfectionism, true OCD involves unwanted thoughts that create severe distress, leading to repetitive behaviors or mental acts to reduce anxiety. It goes beyond wanting things "just right"-it feels like a matter of life and death.

❑ **Just a Personality Trait:** OCD gets confused with personality preferences or quirks. People say, "I'm a bit OCD" about double-checking locks or liking things arranged properly. But OCD interrupts daily life, relationships, and work. It consumes hours of time and creates significant distress.

Common Manifestations

Jessica was a well-established marketing executive who had achieved everything she thought would make her happy—a great career, a loving partner, and a beautiful home. Yet she spent hours each night analyzing text messages from her boyfriend, searching for hidden meanings, questioning his love, and replaying conversations for signs of problems. Her mind turned simple interactions into complex puzzles that needed solving. This pattern, relationship OCD, represents just one way these thought patterns can manifest.

OCD and overthinking show up differently for different people. While Jessica's mind is fixated on relationship doubts, others might find their thoughts stuck on health concerns, moral questions, contamination fears, or the need to check things repeatedly. Let's explore how these common manifestations actually play out in daily life.

Relationship OCD

I am going to use a hypothetical scenario here as an example. We'll use Sarah, who just started dating someone new. Most people might feel butterflies or occasional doubt in a new relationship. But for Sarah, each interaction becomes evidence that needs thorough examination.

When her partner takes an hour to reply to her text, she reads their previous conversation fifteen times, analyzing each word choice. She creates spreadsheets tracking response times, noting changes in how often they use certain phrases or emojis. During dates, instead of being present, she monitors her own feelings constantly: "Am I feeling enough?" "Is this what love should feel like?" "Why did their tone change slightly when talking about weekend plans?"

The need for certainty drives her to seek endless reassurance. She asks friends to analyze conversations, takes online relationship tests, and compares her relationship to others obsessively. Even when her partner explicitly expresses love and commitment, her mind questions the meaning behind the words, searching for hidden signs of doubt or deception.

This constant analysis affects the relationship itself. Spontaneous moments become impossible under such scrutiny. Simple disagreements transform into evidence that the relationship might be wrong. The quest for absolute certainty about love paradoxically makes it harder to experience love fully.

Health Anxiety

Every bodily sensation becomes a potential warning sign when health anxiety takes hold. A mild headache spirals into hours of symptom-checking and urgent doctor visits. That random muscle twitch leads to late-night medical research about neurological conditions. A stomach pain prompts multiple clinic visits, even after doctors find nothing wrong.

Health anxiety goes beyond normal concerns about wellbeing. It creates a constant state of hypervigilance where the body becomes a source of threat rather than a trusted ally. Normal physical sensations most people would ignore become evidence of potential disaster.

Medical information, instead of providing relief, often makes things worse. Each new article or medical website suggests more conditions to worry about. Reassurance from doctors provides only temporary comfort before doubt creeps back in. The very act of monitoring the body so intensely creates new physical symptoms; tension headaches, upset stomach, and muscle pain, which then fuel further health fears.

Even knowing this pattern exists doesn't break its hold. The fear feels too real, the need for certainty too strong, and the possibility of missing something too risky to ignore.

Moral OCD

Moral OCD is the constant questioning of your character, your actions, and your very nature as a person. It latches onto your deepest values and turns them into sources of torment. While most people move past their mistakes or occasional unkind thoughts, moral OCD transforms these into evidence of being fundamentally flawed or evil.

The mind becomes a relentless moral detective, searching through memories for signs of wrongdoing while questioning current actions and even thoughts themselves. A fleeting angry thought about a loved one leads to hours of self-examination. The automatic thought "I hope they fail" about a competitor creates days of worry about being secretly evil. Even religious or spiritual practices transform from sources of comfort into new areas for moral scrutiny-did you pray sincerely enough? Are your motivations for helping others truly pure? What makes it particularly challenging is how it attaches to genuine values. The person experiencing it often cares deeply about being good, kind, and ethical, yet this very concern becomes the source of their torment. Simple decisions become moral dilemmas, casual interactions turn into opportunities for wrongdoing, and the quest for certainty about one's character never ends.

Contamination Fears

Contamination OCD is the kind that turns everyday objects and situations into sources of perceived danger. The sufferer creates strict rules about what's "safe" to touch or be near. A person might refuse to use public bathrooms, avoid shaking hands, or spend hours washing after touching money.

The cleaning rituals become increasingly specific. Someone might wash their hands with hot water for exactly three minutes, then cold water for two minutes, using precisely three pumps of soap. If they lose count or get interrupted, they must start over. Breaking these rules triggers intense anxiety and fear of disaster.

These rituals expand over time. What starts as extra handwashing might grow to include:

❑ Showering multiple times daily

❑ Washing groceries before storing them

❑ Keeping "outdoor" and "indoor" clothes strictly separated

❑ Requiring visitors to follow complex cleaning procedures

❑ Avoiding entire categories of objects or places

Each new rule promises safety but actually restricts life further while demanding more time for rituals. A simple errand like buying milk might require an hour of preparation and clean up afterward.

The Role of Uncertainty

It is very important that we learn how to sit with discomfort, with uncertainty, with the not-knowing. However, when you have OCD, uncertainty usually feels like an emergency that must be resolved immediately; the mind demands answers, guarantees, and absolute certainty that everything will be okay.

Think about the questions that OCD asks: "Are you absolutely sure the door is locked?" "Can you guarantee you won't harm someone?" "Do you know with complete certainty that this isn't contaminated?" When you look closer, they seem to demand perfect answers, but life rarely offers perfect certainty.

Most people can walk away from a locked door thinking "I'm pretty sure I locked it." They can wash their hands once and feel "clean enough." They can make decisions with "good enough" certainty. But OCD hijacks this natural tolerance for uncertainty. It convinces you that anything less than 100% certainty puts you or others at risk.

This intolerance for uncertainty drives the cycle; you check the stove to be certain it's off. But certainty feels temporary. So you check again, and again. Each check actually increases doubt rather than providing lasting relief. The more you seek perfect certainty, the more elusive it becomes, until uncertainty itself feels dangerous.

Breaking free starts with learning to carry uncertainty rather than trying to eliminate it. This doesn't mean being reckless or careless. It means developing the ability to act effectively even when absolute certainty isn't available.

Checking Behaviors

A few years ago I watched a documentary about someone with OCD. They would check their front door lock seventeen times before leaving home. If someone interrupted them during these checks, they had to start over from the beginning. What caught my attention wasn't just the number of checks, but the visible distress when they couldn't complete their ritual exactly right.

Checking behaviors in OCD transforms normal safety measures into elaborate systems that must be performed perfectly. A person might check:

❏ The stove knobs are in a specific order

❏ Each window multiple times, touching the lock a certain way

❏ Email messages for accidental offensive content

❏ Car doors while counting to a specific number

❏ Important documents repeatedly for mistakes

Each check promises relief but actually strengthens doubt. The mind says, "Just one more time" but that one more time never satisfies. The brief relief after checking quickly fades, replaced by nagging uncertainty that drives the next check.

The cost goes beyond time. Relationships strain when others must wait through checking rituals. Work suffers when documents need endless review. Sleep suffers when midnight brings the urge to verify everything again. Simple tasks become marathon sessions of verification, each check feeding the need for another.

WHY TRADITIONAL APPROACHES FALL SHORT

Most advice about intrusive thoughts misses how your brain actually works. Think about what happens when someone tells you "Don't think about a pink elephant." Suddenly, that's exactly what fills your mind. The same thing happens with intrusive thoughts—trying to stop them makes them grow stronger and more persistent.

When you seek reassurance by checking locks repeatedly or asking others for comfort, your brain gets a quick hit of relief. But this relief teaches your brain a dangerous lesson: that these fears need constant checking. Each time you check, the relief gets shorter while the need for certainty grows stronger. Your brain starts demanding more proof, more checking, more reassurance.

Even perfect logic can't touch these patterns. You might know exactly how many germs live on a doorknob or understand the statistical impossibility of your fear coming true. But this knowledge doesn't reach the part of your brain driving these behaviors. It's like trying to fix a computer's hardware by changing its wallpaper-you're working at the wrong level.

Exercise: Drawing Your Thought Pattern

Sometimes seeing a thought from the outside helps us understand it differently. Let's create a visual map of how your thought moves.

On Your Paper:

1. Draw a circle in the center–this is your thought
2. Around it, draw what happens next:
   - ❑ What emotions appear? (Use colors or symbols)
   - ❑ Where does your mind go? (Draw arrows)
   - ❑ What urges show up? (Add shapes)
   - ❑ How does your body react? (Mark locations)

Now Add Labels:

❑ Time of day: _____

❑ Situation: _____

❑ Intensity level: _____

Notes About Your Drawing:

❑ What stands out most: _____

❑ Pattern you notice: _____

❑ Something unexpected: _____

We can't turn our thoughts off or control what appears in our minds, but what we can do is learn to carry them differently; to understand their patterns, their demands for certainty, and their tendency to tighten their grip; these actions give us a map for navigating our minds more skillfully. In the chapters ahead I will show you practical ways to work with these patterns rather than against them, to move forward even when thoughts persist.

Chapter Two

DEFUSING THOUGHTS COMPREHENSIVELY

One of my closest friends is a kindergarten teacher, and she shared this memory trick she teaches her kids called "The Thought Monster Game." When worries show up, her students turn them into silly monsters with squeaky voices. "I'm scared of my presentation" becomes "I'M SCARED OF MY PRESENTATION" in a high-pitched squeal, complete with googly eyes and rainbow hair.

For these five-year-olds, it works like magic. A thought that felt huge and scary transforms into something they can laugh at. "My drawing isn't good" in a Muppet voice just doesn't pack the same punch as the original stern critic in their heads. They learn, without realizing it, that thoughts are just thoughts—not facts, not commands, not absolute truths.

This wisdom from the kindergarten classroom holds something valuable for all of us. When thoughts hook us—when we're caught in loops of overthinking or stuck in OCD patterns—we forget we have options. We forget we can relate to our thoughts differently. But just like those kindergarteners, we can learn to create some space between us and the noise in our heads.

This chapter shows you how to do exactly that.

UNDERSTANDING DEFUSION

Defusion is learning how to recognize thoughts as just thoughts. When anxiety finds you, your mind might say, "Everything's going to go wrong." When fused with this thought, it feels completely true, and your body responds with full panic, but through it, you learn to see it differently: "I'm having the thought that everything's going to go wrong."

This small shift creates space between you and the thought. Rather than being caught in every worried thought, every self-criticism, and every OCD spike, you learn to observe these mental events without being controlled by them. Just like watching cars pass on a street; you can notice them without having to jump into every vehicle.

This differs from positive thinking or thought-stopping. Those approaches try to fight or change thoughts. Defusion simply changes your relationship with thoughts. You'll still have worried thoughts, self-doubt, and OCD spikes. But you'll carry them differently, with more flexibility and less struggle.

CORE DEFUSION TECHNIQUES

Your thoughts shape how you experience reality. When caught in thought loops, a simple worry transforms into absolute truth. An intrusive thought becomes a command that demands action. A self-criticism feels like an unchangeable fact about who you are.

Defusion techniques help break this spell. Not by fighting thoughts or trying to make them go away, but by changing how we relate to them. These practical tools help create space between you and the mental noise, allowing you to see thoughts as mental events rather than facts you must believe or act on.

Let's explore specific techniques that make this shift possible:

Changing How You Carry Thoughts

Persistent thoughts, especially self-critical ones, often feel heavy and true. This technique helps shift their weight by changing how we voice them. Instead of carrying "I'm not good enough" in your usual mental voice—the one that sounds authoritative and convincing-try expressing it differently.

Choose a voice that naturally creates some distance: perhaps a news announcer, a character from your favorite show, or even a different accent. The key lies not in making the thought silly, but in changing how it sounds in your mind. When you shift from your normal mental voice to a different one, the thought often loses some of its perceived authority.

Here's how to practice:

❏ Notice a thought that keeps returning

❏ Observe how it usually sounds in your mind

❏ Choose a different voice-one that feels natural to you

❏ Express the thought in this new voice

❏ Notice any shifts in how the thought feels

The goal is to experience thoughts differently, creating enough distance to work with them more effectively.

The Stream of Thoughts Practice

Your mind produces thousands of thoughts daily. Some demand attention, creating distress until you respond. This practice teaches you to step back and observe the natural flow of thinking.

First, start by bringing attention to your breath and finding a steady, comfortable rhythm. Picture a scene in nature that feels calming; perhaps a mountain stream, ocean waves, or leaves in the wind. Let this image become clear in your mind.

As thoughts arise, imagine placing them in this natural flow. A worry about work joins the movement. A memory from yesterday enters the scene. A thought about dinner flows through. No need to chase thoughts or push them away. Simply watch their natural movement.

Through this, you will build a different relationship with thinking. Rather than getting caught in every thought, you learn to observe their coming and going with more ease.

Acknowledging Your Mind's Protection

When worry floods in, most of us either argue with our thoughts or try to push them away. Both strategies drain our energy while making thoughts return stronger. The "Thank You, Mind" practice transforms this struggle by acknowledging your mind's protective intent.

When difficult thoughts arise, respond with "Thank you, mind, for trying to keep me safe." This simple phrase shifts your relationship with anxiety, OCD, and overthinking. Instead of viewing these thoughts as problems to solve, you recognize them as your mind's attempt at protection. Even when its methods create more distress than safety, your mind sends these warnings because it wants to help.

Practice this acknowledgment with smaller worries first. Notice how accepting your mind's protective role feels different from fighting against it. This shift creates space to work differently with difficult thoughts.

Working with Worry

Worry hijacks your mind with vivid scenes of everything that could go wrong. Your presentation next week becomes a guaranteed disaster. That slight pain must be a serious illness. Your child's late return from school spawns scenarios of accidents. Each worry feels urgent, demanding immediate attention and problem-solving.

Defusion helps break worry's grip by changing how you respond to these thoughts. Instead of diving into each disaster scenario, trying to solve it or prove it won't happen, practice noticing: "Here's my mind doing its worry thing." When you catch yourself planning responses to imagined disasters, label it: "I'm having the thought that everything will go wrong."

Start with smaller worries to build this skill. When your mind offers a worried thought about being late to work, instead of immediately engaging with all the potential consequences, practice saying: "I notice I'm having thoughts about being late." Feel the difference between being caught in the worry versus observing it.

Real problems deserve attention and planning, and with this, you'll be able to distinguish between productive problem-solving and mental scenarios that only increase anxiety. This skill allows you to respond thoughtfully rather than reacting to every potential disaster your mind creates.

Handling Self-Criticism

Self-critical thoughts feel especially true because they come in your own voice. Externalizing them removes their power: notice "There goes my mind with old doubts" instead of identifying with those doubts completely. This creates breathing room between you and harsh self-judgments.

Like learning to hold a hot mug by its handle rather than grasping the heated surface directly, practicing distance from critical thoughts lets you acknowledge them without being burned by them. You remain aware of their presence while choosing whether to let them direct your actions.

Notice when your inner voice turns harsh. You can observe "Ah, there's that familiar self-criticism," the same way you might notice clouds passing overhead-present but not permanent, seen but not necessarily believed.

Breaking Rumination Cycles

Rumination is mental stuck-ness. Your mind latches onto a thought, event, or problem and refuses to let go. It analyzes the same situation repeatedly, seeking perfect understanding or trying to prevent future mistakes. Like a record player with its needle stuck in a groove, rumination keeps you replaying the same mental track.

Let's practice working with rumination:

Find a quiet space and take 10 minutes. Write down one thought your mind keeps circling back to lately. Notice how long this thought has been playing on repeat, what brings it back, what keeps it going. Now set a timer for 5 minutes. Each time this thought appears, label it: "Here's rumination about [topic]." Make a note of when it shows up, then gently return your attention to your breath or surroundings.

Keep a simple daily log for a week, then notice when rumination starts, how long it lasts, and what helps you step back. This builds awareness of your rumination patterns and strengthens your ability to notice them without getting caught up in analysis. The goal isn't stopping rumination but learning to carry these thoughts differently.

Practice this exercise daily. Start with shorter periods if needed. Notice what changes as you build this skill of stepping back from mental loops.

TRACKING THOUGHT INTENSITY: A DEFUSION LOG

Our thoughts shift and change when we learn to relate to them differently. By tracking one persistent thought over a week, you'll discover patterns in how defusion techniques affect its intensity and impact. Choose a thought that shows up regularly but isn't your most challenging one—this helps you practice with something manageable.

Choose One Persistent Thought: _____

Notice how this thought typically affects you before starting defusion work.

DAY 1

Morning Check-in

Write down your thought's current intensity (1-10): _____.

Describe any physical sensations in your body:

_____

_____

Which defusion technique will you try today:

_____

_____

What happened when you used the technique:

_____

_____

_____

_____

Evening Review

How did your relationship with the thought change today:

Which moments of practice felt most helpful:

What made practice challenging:

DAY 2

Morning Check-in

Write down your thought's current intensity (1-10): -------------

Describe any physical sensations in your body:

Which defusion technique will you try today:

What happened when you used the technique:

Evening Review

How did your relationship with the thought change today:

_____

_____

Which moments of practice felt most helpful:

_____

_____

What made practice challenging:

_____

_____

Tracking Thought Intensity: A Week of Defusion

Our thoughts shift and change when we learn to relate to them differently. By tracking one persistent thought over a week, you'll discover patterns in how defusion techniques affect its intensity and impact. Choose a thought that shows up regularly but isn't your most challenging one—this helps you practice with something manageable.

Choose One Persistent Thought: _____

Notice how this thought typically affects you before starting defusion work.

DAY 3

Morning Check-in

Write down your thought's current intensity (1-10): _____

Describe any physical sensations in your body:

_____

_____

Which defusion technique will you try today:

_____

What happened when you used the technique:

_____

_____

Evening Review

How did your relationship with the thought change today:

_____

_____

Which moments of practice felt most helpful:

_____

_____

What made practice challenging:

_____

_____

DAY 4

Morning Check-in

Write down your thought's current intensity (1-10): _____

Describe any physical sensations in your body:

_____

_____

Which defusion technique will you try today:

_____

What happened when you used the technique:

_____

_____

Evening Review

How did your relationship with the thought change today:

_____

_____

Which moments of practice felt most helpful:

_____

_____

What made practice challenging:

_____

_____

DAY 5

Morning Check-in

Write down your thought's current intensity (1-10): _____.

Describe any physical sensations in your body:

_____

_____

Which defusion technique will you try today:

_____

What happened when you used the technique:

_____

_____

Evening Review

How did your relationship with the thought change today:

_____

_____

Which moments of practice felt most helpful:

_____

_____

What made practice challenging:

_____

_____

DAY 6

Morning Check-in

Write down your thought's current intensity (1-10): _____

Describe any physical sensations in your body:

_____

_____

Which defusion technique will you try today:

_____

What happened when you used the technique:

_____

_____

Evening Review

How did your relationship with the thought change today:

_____

_____

Which moments of practice felt most helpful:

_____

_____

What made practice challenging:

_____

_____

DAY 7

Morning Check-in

Write down your thought's current intensity (1-10): _____.

Describe any physical sensations in your body:

_____

_____

Which defusion technique will you try today:

_____

What happened when you used the technique:

_____

_____

Evening Review

How did your relationship with the thought change today:

_____

_____

Which moments of practice felt most helpful:

_____

_____

What made practice challenging:

_____

_____

BREAKING THE RUMINATION CYCLE: A PRACTICE EXERCISE

Rumination keeps us stuck in mental loops, replaying past events or worrying about future scenarios. This exercise helps you identify when you're caught in rumination and offers concrete steps to shift your attention. Take time with each step, noting your responses honestly.

Step 1: Catch the Loop

Notice when you're stuck in repetitive thoughts. Write down:

The situation triggering rumination: _____

How long you've been thinking about it: _____

What your mind keeps returning to: _____

Step 2: Physical Check-in

Your body often signals rumination before your mind notices:

Where do you feel tension?: _____

What sensations are strongest?: _____

How has your breathing changed?: _____

Step 3: Identify the Hook

What keeps this thought cycle going: _____

What answer is your mind seeking?: _____

What feels unresolved?: _____

What are you trying to prevent?: _____

Step 4: Choose Your Response

Instead of staying caught in the loop:_____

One small action you can take now: _____

Where can you redirect your attention: _____

What helps you return to the present: _____

Practice Notes

Time of day: _____

What worked best: _____

What you learned: _____

You will need to go at this consistently, each time you notice and redirect your attention, you build the skill of disengaging from mental loops.

You can try to control your thoughts, to seek perfect mastery of your mind. I've watched so many people exhaust themselves in this battle—arguing with every anxious thought, questioning every doubt, fighting against their own humanity. But thoughts move like rivers flow, as seasons change. The techniques in this chapter offer something different: ways to stand steady while thoughts pass through, to carry even the heaviest thoughts with more grace. You'll still have difficult thoughts, still face uncertainty, and still encounter mental storms. But you'll meet them differently, with more space to choose your path forward.

Chapter Three

MINDFULNESS FOR MENTAL CLARITY

I love to walk, I love to listen to my thoughts when I wander through my neighborhood at dusk. Each footstep brings its own rhythm, its own clarity. The mind naturally settles into this movement, like water finding its level. I notice this most on days when thoughts feel tangled—when work problems loop endlessly, when anxiety creates static, and when OCD demands certainty.

Walking shows me something about clarity—how it comes not from forcing thoughts to behave but from finding steady ground beneath them. The thoughts might still swirl, but I've learned to feel my feet on the earth, to let evening air fill my lungs, to notice how even racing thoughts eventually settle like leaves after wind.

Years ago, a therapist asked me what I did when my thoughts became too loud. I told her about these walks, and about how movement helped me find space around difficult thoughts. "That's mindfulness," she said. "You've found your way back to the present moment." She was right, but she also showed me how to bring that same quality of attention to other moments—sitting at my desk, stuck in traffic, lying awake at night.

This chapter explores how to find that kind of clarity, even when you can't take a walk at dusk. These tools work with your brain's natural capacity for awareness, helping you return to steady ground when thoughts create storms. Let me show you how to build this practice into your daily life.

BUILDING MENTAL CLARITY

My grandmother used to say that 'a cluttered mind makes everything harder.' She'd start each day sorting her thoughts like she sorted her kitchen; keeping only what served her, letting go of what didn't. She taught me that mental clarity comes through small daily practices, through regular habits of noticing and releasing what clouds our thinking.

Mental clarity requires understanding what compromises the constant analysis of every decision. The need to control uncertain outcomes. The habit of rehearsing conversations or replaying events. Each person's mind gets clouded in particular ways. Recognizing your patterns marks the first step toward clearing them.

This section explores practical tools for building mental clarity—not through controlling thoughts, but through strengthening your ability to see clearly even when thoughts create noise.

Understanding What Clouds Thinking

Mental clarity suffers when multiple factors pile up in our minds. Overthinking turns simple decisions into complex puzzles that feel impossible to solve. Analysis of past events keeps us stuck reviewing what we can't change. The drive to control future outcomes creates constant planning and worry. Self-monitoring makes us hyper-aware of every thought and feeling. Add in the constant stream of information from devices and media, plus physical factors like poor sleep or nutrition, and our minds become increasingly clouded.

Our perspective, as we've learned, is not always the most reliable source of information. Three key factors often distort our thinking:

❑ **Unconscious Biases:** These color in how we interpret situations and make decisions. We might favor information that confirms what we already believe, or remember only the details that support our current mood.

❑ **Memory Distortion:** Our memories shift and change over time, so what feels like a clear recollection often contains gaps our minds fill with assumptions. This especially affects how we remember emotional events or conversations.

❑ **Stress Impact:** When stress levels rise, our thinking narrows. Complex situations appear in black and white. Neutral events feel threatening. Our ability to see multiple perspectives diminishes just when we need it most.

Reconnecting with the Present Moment

When thoughts take over, you need concrete actions to break their momentum. Stop whatever you're doing and deliberately place both feet flat on the floor. Press your hands against your thighs, feeling the pressure and temperature. Take one full breath, noticing the entire cycle of inhaling and exhaling. Look around and name three specific things you can see right now.

This combination of deliberate physical movement and sensory awareness pulls attention from mental chatter into direct experience. Practice this reset during natural pauses in your day; work breaks, traffic lights, before important conversations. Regular practice helps it become automatic when thoughts start racing.

This differs from vague instructions to "be present" or "stay mindful." Specific physical actions and sensory focus make reconnecting with the present moment tangible rather than abstract.

Using Your Senses as Anchors

Your sense are trustworthy ways back to the present moment; for instance, touch connects you immediately with what's real; place your feet on ground, hands on desk, weight in chair. Sound expands our attention outward, from distant traffic to nearby conversation.

Sight returns you to your actual environment through colors and movement.

Taste and smell often get overlooked but are just as strong anchors. After having eaten or drank someone, allow yourself to connect to the lingering flavor of the coffee, or focus on the scent of fresh air; even the taste of mint gum can pull attention back to now. These intimate senses bypass mental chatter directly. Allow yourself to feel the temperature against your skin. Notice the texture under your fingertips. Listen to the layers of sound around you. Observe light and shadow. Taste what's present in your mouth. Smell the air you're breathing. Each sense offers a different doorway back to the present moment.

Regular practice with all your senses will help you build a stronger support system that will pull you out of overthinking, but work first with one sense at a time until shifting attention from thoughts to physical experience is as natural as breathing.

Daily Sensory Mindfulness Log

Each time you practice using your senses as anchors to the present moment, record your experience here. Notice which senses feel most accessible and which ones help you ground most effectively.

Today's Date: _____

Time of Practice: _____

Touch Practice

What I noticed through touch: _____

Where I felt it most clearly: _____

How it helped ground me: _____

Sound Experience

Sounds I noticed: _____

Most grounding sound: _____

How my attention shifted: _____

Visual Anchors

What I observed: _____

Details that stood out: _____

How seeing clearly helped: _____

Taste/Smell Notes

Flavors or scents present: _____

How they anchored me: _____

What I discovered: _____

Overall Practice Reflection

Most effective sense today: _____

Challenging moments: _____

What I learned: _____

How my overthinking shifted: _____

Tomorrow's Focus

Sense I want to explore more: _____

Time I'll practice: _____

What might help: _____

Each sensory experience offers a different path back to the present moment. Notice which ones work best for you in different situations.

WORKING WITH SPIRALS

A thought spiral happens when one thought leads to another, then another, picking up speed and intensity until you are completely caught up in a loop that you can't seem to escape. It's just like obsessing over a mistake at work until you've convinced yourself you'll get fired, or turning a small pain into a terminal illness through hours of internet research.

Catching Spirals Early

Your body will signal the start of a spiral long before your mind catches up, so keep a look out for the physical signs: shallow breathing, tense muscles, a tight chest, and then notice when your thoughts speed up or start looping on the same theme.

These early warning signs are a chance to intervene before the spiral gains force.

When you notice these signals:

❑ Take one long breath that makes your belly expand. Feel both feet on the ground. Name what's happening in simple terms: "Work worry is starting" or "Health anxiety is kicking in." This brief pause and naming often reduces the spiral's initial momentum.

❑ Check your surroundings. Are you hunched over your phone? Sitting in the dark? Alone with your thoughts for too long? Make one small change to your environment. Turn on a light. Step outside. Call someone who helps you think clearly.

❑ Observe and keep track of when these spirals tend to start. Notice patterns around the time of day, situations, or triggers. This information helps you catch loops earlier each time.

Worksheet: Creating Your Spiral Response Plan

When thought spirals grip your mind, having a clear strategy helps you respond thoughtfully instead of getting swept away. This worksheet guides you through building your personal response plan. Take time with each section, making it specific to your experience with thought spirals.

Understanding Your Signals

Before creating your plan, identify how thought spirals show up in your life. Your body often signals their arrival before your mind notices. Think about your last few spirals:

❑ What physical sensations appeared first? Note where tension showed up, how your breathing changed, and what happened in your stomach or chest.

❑ What emotions emerged? Write down the feelings that preceded or accompanied your spiral.

❑ Which thoughts signaled the start? Track the first few thoughts that began the loop.

Building Your Response Tools

Now let's create specific responses for when you catch these signals:

Immediate Actions

Write three concrete actions you can take within seconds of noticing a spiral:

❑ A physical movement that grounds you: _____

❑ A breathing pattern that helps: _____

❑ Words you'll say to yourself: _____

Environment Shifts

List changes you can make to your surroundings:

❑ What you'll adjust in your space: _____

❑ Where you might move to: _____

❑ How you'll change your physical position: _____

Support System

Identify who can help when spirals intensify:

❑ Person to call for grounding: _____

❑ Professional support available:_____

❑ Places you can go for help: _____

Testing and Refining

Practice this plan for one week. Each time you use it, note:

❑ What worked immediately?
❑ What took more time?
❑ What needs changing?

This plan will be more effective the more you implement it, gradually start with small spirals first, then adapt your approach for more challenging moments.

Breaking the Momentum

Despite what we've been told, I am learning that I cannot think my way out of overthinking. Like trying to use gasoline to put out a fire, using more analysis only feeds the spiral. Breaking free requires immediate action.

Physical actions break mental loops, so another helpful thing to do is to splash cold water on your face until the temperature shock resets your system. Do jumping jacks or push-ups until your breathing changes rhythm. Run up and down stairs until your legs burn. Physical sensation pulls your attention away from spinning thoughts naturally.

Sound shifts thought patterns quickly. Play music with a strong beat that vibrates through your body. Sing out loud, focusing on remembering lyrics. Call a friend to hear their voice say hello.

Hum deeply to feel the vibration in your chest, moving attention to physical sensation.

Move your body to a new space. Walk to a different room with changed lighting or temperature. Step outside to feel the weather on your skin. Drive to a park or coffee shop. Moving your body creates distance from spiraling thoughts.

Simple actions work better and the sooner you move, the faster thoughts shift. Each time you break momentum through action rather than thinking, you build confidence in handling difficult thoughts differently.

Finding Ground

One of my mentors told me that we need to continuously work on establishing truth for ourselves, and by truth, I am referring to the things that are aligned with reality rather than thought-based fears. When caught in mental spirals, we need solid facts to stand on, with what we know for certain, not what we think might happen, not what others have said, but what we can verify right now. To create this, I want you to touch the desk in front of you. Feel the floor under your feet. Name three things you see.

Then observe what your basic needs are. Have you eaten today? How much sleep did you get? When did you last drink water? Physical needs often affect mental stability more than we realize. Address these concrete factors first.

Look for external verification, but not through endless reassurance-seeking, but through clear evidence. If worrying about work performance, look at your actual accomplishments and feedback. If you're caught in relationship anxiety, look at real interactions rather than interpretations. You want to establish a foundation of facts that you can return to when your thoughts try to pull you into speculation or fear; small, verifiable truths create steady ground.

Do you know that feeling that emerges in your chest after you've been in dreary weather for a while and then are finally able to see some sunlight again? When the clouds part and warmth touch your face, and something in you remembers: oh yes, this is also possible. This is what working with mental clarity feels like; not forcing the clouds away, not fighting against storms of thought, but learning to trust that clarity remains even when temporarily obscured. These practices offer ways back to that inner brightness; not through struggling with your mind, but through remembering how to return to what's real, what's true, what's actually here.

Chapter Four

EMBRACING
UNCERTAINTY

My aunt was an adventurous person. During holidays, we'd sit around a table and listen to her regale us with stories of how she'd packed a backpack to travel across South America, armed with basic Spanish and a willingness to figure things out as she went. What struck me most wasn't the adventures themselves, but how comfortable she seemed with not knowing what would happen next.

"The best stories," she'd say, "come from the moments you couldn't plan for." Her entire approach to life taught me something about uncertainty-how it could be a doorway to possibility rather than just a source of anxiety.

Most of us take the opposite approach. We try to plan every detail, research every option, and predict every outcome. We seek certainty like it's a shield that can protect us from discomfort or disappointment. But life has its own plans, its own rhythm of revealing and concealing what comes next.

This chapter takes a little bit of a closer look at how to work differently with uncertainty. Not by conquering it or eliminating it, but by learning to carry it more lightly, to find steady ground even when the path ahead isn't clear.

UNDERSTANDING THE NEED FOR CERTAINTY

Our need for certainty comes from needing safety and knowing that if all else fails, then at least we'll have something solid to stand on. This drive runs deep in our biology, connected to basic survival instincts and our need to predict what comes next.

We spend enormous energy trying to make life predictable, researching every decision until we feel sure. Planning conversations before they happen, creating backup plans for our backup plans. Checking and rechecking until anxiety temporarily subsides. Each attempt at certainty promises safety but paradoxically increases our fear of uncertainty.

The brain treats uncertainty like a threat to our survival; when we can't predict outcomes, our mind activates ancient protective mechanisms, that increase cortisol, and adrenaline because this is a biological response that once protected us from real dangers-predators, weather, food scarcity. But today, these same protective instincts are the same ones that keep us stuck in overthinking and overcontrolling patterns.

Our culture amplifies this biological drive because success is more often than not defined by clear plans and guaranteed outcomes. Doubt is labeled as weakness, and uncertainty as failure. Schools reward students who give definite answers; jobs promote people who project confidence in their decisions, and the media celebrates stories of people who "knew exactly what they wanted." These messages push us toward safe choices and familiar paths, even when they limit our potential.

The Paradox of Uncertainty

My grandfather once told me that if we were always certain of what the outcome would be in any given situation, then we'd rarely ever take risks worth taking. Yet most of us exhaust ourselves trying to guarantee results before we act.

We often chase certainty through research, constant opinion-seeking, and detailed planning. Each action promises to make us feel more secure about what comes next, but what it actually often does is amplify our anxiety. For example, the wedding planner who obsesses over preventing every possible problem creates new worries with each solution; the student who studies obsessively for an exam exhausts themselves into poor performance, and the person checking their phone repeatedly for a response invited anxiety to spike with each and every check because one leads to another. One person's reassurance demands verification from someone else; one backup plan spawns three more. We create loops of certainty-seeking that actually prevent us from moving forward.

We forget through all of this that life's most meaningful choices are the ones that require \us to act without perfect knowledge. Jobs change, relationships evolve, opportunities appear without guarantee, and waiting for complete certainty keeps us stuck while life moves forward. The path to growth opens when we learn to act alongside uncertainty rather than demanding its elimination.

Building Tolerance Toward Uncertainty

To be with life in all its beautiful forms, we must learn how to relinquish control, to accept that sometimes we won't know and that is ok. We must accept that acting, despite having all the necessary information is part of being human. Let me show you five practical ways to build your tolerance for uncertainty.

❑ **Accept and Acknowledge:** Stop fighting against not knowing. When uncertainty arises, name it directly: "I don't know what will happen next, and that's making me anxious." This acknowledgment often reduces the power of uncertainty over your actions. Practice saying "I don't know" without immediately trying to solve or fix the situation. Let yourself feel the discomfort of uncertainty rather than rushing to eliminate it.

❑ **Build Flexible Knowledge:** Gather information without seeking perfect certainty. Research enough to make informed choices, but recognize when more information stops being helpful. Ask yourself: "Do I need more knowledge, or am I seeking impossible guarantees?" Set time limits on research. Make decisions with the information you have rather than waiting for complete certainty.

❑ **Develop Flexible Thinking:** Practice holding multiple possibilities at once. Instead of demanding to know exactly how something will turn out, explore different potential outcomes. When your mind insists on knowing "the answer," remind yourself that most situations have multiple valid paths forward. Challenge black-and-white thinking by finding the gray areas in situations.

❑ **Create a Healthy Relationship with Threat:** Learn to distinguish between real and imagined threats. Question your mind's worst-case scenarios. Most uncertainties we fear never materialize, yet we let them stop us from moving forward. Track your feared outcomes versus actual results to build evidence of your ability to handle uncertainty.

❑ **Practice Rational Problem-Solving:** Focus on what you can influence rather than what you can't control. Break the larger uncertainties into smaller, manageable steps. Take action on the parts within your power while accepting what remains unknown. Create specific action plans for the aspects you can affect, while practicing acceptance of what remains uncertain.

The Worst-Case Scenario Exercise

Most of us avoid looking directly at our fears about uncertainty, we push away worst-case scenarios, hoping that not thinking about them will make them less likely to happen. But this avoidance actually increases their power over us. Let's try something different.

Take out a piece of paper. Write down your current uncertainty: a relationship, a job change, a health concern. Now, instead of pushing away the fears, let's look at them directly:

❑ Write your worst-case scenario in detail.

❑ List exactly how you would cope if it happened.

❑ Write down the skills and resources you already have.

❑ Note who could help you through it.

❑ Look at how you've handled difficult situations before.

This exercise shows you two important things: First, that even worst-case scenarios have specific solutions. Second, you have more capability to handle uncertainty than your fear suggests. Practice this whenever uncertainty feels overwhelming. Each time you face your fears directly, they lose some of their power to control your actions.

Finding Peace in Maybe

Most of us hate "maybe." We want yes or no, right or wrong, certain or impossible. But life lives in maybe. Maybe that job will work out. Maybe that relationship will grow stronger. Maybe things will be harder than expected, or maybe they'll unfold more beautifully than we imagined.

Try this experiment: For one day, replace your need to know with "maybe." When anxiety pushes for certainty about a situation, respond with "Maybe it will work out, maybe it won't." When OCD demands guarantees, answer with "Maybe that could happen." When overthinking tries to solve every possibility, return to "maybe I don't need to figure this out right now."

You are not spending your whole day dismissing real concerns, what you're doing is loosening your grip on needing to know. Each "maybe" creates space where certainty once squeezed all the air out of the room. Each "maybe" lets you take action without demanding guarantees.

Let "maybe" be a reminder that you can handle what comes, even if you can't predict it perfectly.

It is safer to feel and welcome uncertainty when we stop fixating on perfection, predictions, or promises of guaranteed outcomes. Life moves in unexpected ways-relationships deepen through surprises, careers unfold through unplanned opportunities, and growth happens in moments we could never design. When we loosen our grip on needing to know, something shifts. We start saying yes to experiences our fear of uncertainty once kept us from. We find strength in situations we used to avoid. We learn to trust, not that everything will work out perfectly, but that we can handle what comes next.

Chapter Five

LIVING BEYOND LOOPS

There is an African proverb that says when you are lost in the forest, look to the tallest tree for direction. For generations, travelers would seek these natural landmarks when paths disappeared under fallen leaves or darkness made familiar signs hard to read. The tallest tree became their constant guide, helping them find their way back to their village, their families, and their homes.

In my work with people caught in mental loops, I've watched them find similar guidance through their values. The mother, overwhelmed by health anxiety remembered the value of being present with her children. The student paralyzed by perfectionism who reconnected with his love of learning. The businessman trapped in a relationship overthinking returned to his core value of genuine connection. Their values, like those tallest trees, showed them a way forward when their minds made everything seem unclear.

Our minds create elaborate protective systems that end up limiting us. We analyze every word of a conversation to prevent rejection, yet lose our ability to connect naturally. We plan every detail of a presentation to avoid failure, but anxiety steals our capacity to speak from the heart. We check our bodies constantly for signs of illness while missing the simple experience of feeling alive. Each loop promises safety but delivers only distance from what matters most.

Values guide us back. Not through perfect answers or complete certainty, but by reminding us what we want our lives to stand for beyond our fears. They show us what's worth moving toward even when our minds get noisy with doubt.

THE DIFFERENCE BETWEEN GOALS AND VALUES

Values guide our daily choices and actions by providing a compass rather than a destination. While goals like promotions or achievements can be checked off, values like growth, connection, or creativity shape how we move through each moment. They answer the "how" and "why" behind our actions:

Growth value: Brings curiosity to both successes and setbacks Connection value: Creates meaningful moments in all interactions Health value: Guides choices about movement and self-care

When making decisions, values offer clear direction by asking "What matters most here?" rather than "What's the perfect outcome?" They help us choose actions aligned with what we care about, even when the path feels uncertain.

EXPLORING AND IDENTIFYING CORE PERSONAL VALUES

Having values is really what has pulled me out of some of the stickiest situations of my life. Like one time during college when anxiety about my future career paralyzed me completely. I spent hours researching every possible path, analyzing every potential outcome, and trying to guarantee I wouldn't make a mistake. My mind created elaborate charts comparing options, pros and cons lists that stretched for pages, and scenarios that branched endlessly into the future.

Then my mentor asked me a simple question: "Beyond success or security, what matters to you most?" This cut through the noise.

My value of creativity, of making things that help others, had guided me long before career anxiety took over. This value didn't tell me exactly which path to take, but it showed me how to move forward despite uncertainty.

Values shine brightest in moments of confusion. When mental loops trap us in analysis, when fear pushes for perfect answers, when doubt makes every choice feel dangerous, values remind us what we want our lives to stand for.

Let me show you how to find yours.

Personal Values

Our personal values are the ones that guide us in moments when our minds get too noisy to think clearly. They show up naturally in joy, in choices we're proud of, in moments when we feel most alive. Most of the time, you find that they're already present in how we move through life when we're at our best.

They show up show up differently for everyone. For some, connection means deep one-on-one conversations. For others, it means building community or strengthening family bonds. Growth for one person can be a formal education for one person, while another finds it in life experiences and challenges. Creativity appears not just in art, but in problem-solving, cooking, or how someone runs their business.

Let's explore some common values that guide people's lives, not as a checklist to choose from, but as a starting point to recognize what already matters most to you:

❑ authenticity	❑ courage	❑ contribution
❑ connection	❑ compassion	❑ learning
❑ growth	❑ adventure	❑ family
❑ creativity	❑ peace	❑ independence

❏ health   ❏ community   ❏ integrity

❏ justice   ❏ excellence   ❏ joy

❏ spirituality   ❏ wisdom

Finding Your Values: A Personal Exploration

Find a quiet hour and then bring a journal, something to drink, and an openness to discover what matters most to you. This isn't about right answers-it's about uncovering what already guides you when you're at your best.

Start with life's highlight reel. Write down:

A moment you felt incredibly proud.

A time you lost track of time because you were so engaged.

A decision that felt absolutely right despite being difficult.

A memory that still makes you smile when you think about it.

Notice what these moments share. What qualities were you expressing? What mattered to you in those times? These patterns point toward your core values.

Now reflect on these questions:

What would you still do even if no one ever knew about it?

What makes you feel most alive?

What would you stand up for even if others disagreed?

What kind of person do you want to be, beyond any specific achievement?

Look for themes in your answers. Maybe courage keeps appearing, or creativity, or connection with others. Write down every value that resonates strongly.

Finally, narrow your list to 5-7 core values. These aren't the only ones that matter, but they're your current north stars. For each one, write:

What this value means specifically to you?

How you already express it in your life?

One small way you could live it more fully tomorrow.

PROFESSIONAL VALUES

Step back to your most fulfilling work moments. Maybe it was finishing a challenging project that helped others, mentoring someone who now excels, or solving a problem everyone thought impossible. What made these moments matter? What qualities were you expressing?

Find quiet time with your journal and reflect on:

❑ A work achievement you're genuinely proud of

❑ A problem you loved solving

❑ A day that flew by because you were so engaged

❑ A professional relationship that taught you something valuable

❑ A challenge that helped you grow

Now dig deeper with these questions:

❑ What parts of your work would you do even if no one noticed?

❑ When do you lose track of time at work?

❑ What problems draw you in completely?

❑ What do colleagues consistently thank you for?

❑ What skills do you enjoy developing?

Common Professional Values include:

❑ Excellence: Creating work that meets your standards

❑ Innovation: Finding fresh solutions to old problems

❑ Leadership: Helping others reach their potential

❑ Integrity: Staying true to principles under pressure

❑ Impact: Seeing your work makes a real difference

❑ Collaboration: Building something greater together

❑ Autonomy: Freedom to work in your own way

❑ Growth: Continuous learning and development

❑ Balance: Sustainable success

❑ Creativity: Bringing new ideas to life

Take time with each value that resonates. Write:

❑ How you've expressed this value in past work

❑ Where you see opportunities to express it more

❑ Small ways to bring it into tomorrow's tasks

Choose 5-7 core professional values. These will be your compass for career decisions and daily work choices.

Creating Your Values Map

A values map shows you where you're heading versus where you want to go in key life areas. This practical tool helps align daily choices with what matters most to you. By examining different areas of life separately, you can see patterns more clearly and make specific changes rather than getting overwhelmed by trying to change everything at once.

Key Life Areas to Map:

❑ Work/Career includes your professional growth, daily tasks, workplace relationships, and long-term aspirations. Look at how your values show up (or don't) in meetings, projects, and interactions with colleagues.

❑ Relationships/Family covers connections with partners, family, and close friends. Examine how you show up in important conversations, during conflicts, and in daily interactions.

❑ Personal Growth encompasses learning, spiritual development, and emotional maturity. Consider how you handle challenges, what you're learning, and how you're developing.

❑ Health/Physical Wellbeing looks at exercise, nutrition, rest, and body care. Notice your daily habits, energy levels, and how you treat your body.

❑ Community/Social Life involves your role in larger groups, contributions to others, and social connections. Consider how you engage with your community and build meaningful relationships.

❑ Leisure/Recreation examines how you recharge, what brings you joy, how you spend your free time. Look at whether your recreational choices align with your value.

The Mapping Exercise:

Step 1: Rate Current Direction. For each life area, rate (1-10) how closely your current actions match your values. Example:

❑ If you value creativity at work but spend most days on routine tasks: 3/10

❑ If you value family connection and make time for it daily: 8/10

Step 2: Set Desired Direction. Write specifically how you want to express your values in each area. Example:

❑ Work: Using creativity to solve problems, mentoring others

❑ Family: Having meaningful conversations, being fully present

Step 3: Note the Gaps. Identify where current actions don't match the desired direction. Be specific:

❑ Work: Spend 80% of the time on admin, and only 20% on creative projects

❑ Health: Value vitality but skip exercise most days

Step 4: Plan Small Steps. Choose one action per area to better align with your values:

❑ Work: Dedicate the first hour to creative tasks

❑ Health: Ten-minute walk during lunch break

VALUES IN ACTION TRACKER

Track how your daily choices align with your core values. Notice opportunities to express your values even in small moments.

Today's Date:

Morning Check-in

Value focusing on today: -------------------------------------

Opportunities I see ahead: -------------------------------------

Potential challenges: -------------------------------------

Value-Based Choices Made

Morning:

Situation: -------------------------------------

Value expressed: -------------------------------------

How it felt: -------------------------------------

Afternoon:

Situation: -------------------------------------

Value expressed: -------------------------------------

How it felt: -------------------------------------

Evening:

Situation: -------------------------------------

Value expressed: -------------------------------------

How it felt: -------------------------------------

Reflection

Most aligned moment today: _____

Missed opportunities: _____

What I learned: _____

Tomorrow's Focus

Value to emphasize: _____

Specific situations to watch for: _____

Support I need: _____

Weekly Review

Values expressed most: _____

New opportunities noticed: _____

Areas for growth: _____

Next week's focus: _____

Remember: Small choices build patterns. Each value-aligned action strengthens your connection to what matters most.

Sometimes our values face their toughest tests precisely when they matter most. That promotion might challenge your value of integrity. A relationship might test your commitment to authenticity. Health issues might strain your value of courage. In these moments, values don't make choices easier-they make them clearer. They remind us what we want to stand for, even when standing there feels difficult.

Our values might shift as we grow, as life teaches us new lessons, and as we understand ourselves more deeply. What mattered at twenty might differ from what mattered at forty. But this changing nature of values doesn't make them less reliable-it makes them more real. The key lies not in holding rigidly to past values or rushing to find new ones, but in staying connected to what feels genuinely true right now. Values guide us best when we let them grow with us, when we check in regularly to make sure they still resonate, and when we allow them to deepen and evolve as we do. This journey toward living aligned with your values starts now, with each small choice that moves you closer to what feels authentically true.

Conclusion

Some time ago, I went bungee jumping and it was the scariest moment of my life. My heart, at the time, felt like it was pounding from outside my chest. Standing at that edge, every instinct screamed to step back, to choose safety, to avoid the terror of letting go. My mind raced with reasons to walk away-statistics about accidents, worries about the equipment, and thoughts about my family. But something deeper than fear pulled me forward. Not courage exactly, but a knowing that these But something deeper than fear compelled me to move forward. It wasn't exactly courage, but rather an understanding that these moments—when fear feels the most overwhelming—are the most significant.

Working with difficult thoughts asks for this same kind of trust. Not in bungee cords or safety equipment, but in your capacity to carry uncertainty, to feel fear without letting it stop you, to move toward what matters even when your mind fills with doubt. The tools in this book won't eliminate hard thoughts or difficult feelings. They offer something better-a way to build a life guided by your values rather than your fears, to find freedom not in perfect certainty but in the willingness to live fully even when thoughts get loud.

Book Four

BREAKING ANXIETY'S GRIP

ACT-Based Strategies to Conquer Fear,
Find Courage, and Align with Your Values

Introduction

I knew that I was healing when I finally allowed myself to be okay with things not being perfect, when I no longer felt the need to play, predict and control every aspect of my life. Anxiety thrives on our fear of uncertainty, pushing us to seek control where none exists. Like trying to grip water, the tighter we hold, the more slips through our fingers.

It happened on an ordinary Tuesday afternoon, as I watched autumn leaves scatter across my backyard. A simple moment, really. The wind picked up, sending the leaves into a chaotic dance, and instead of feeling that familiar tightness in my chest—that urge to somehow control their movement—I just watched. For the first time in years, I breathed easily.

Pause here for a moment. What fear have you been trying to control? What would it feel like to loosen your grip, even slightly? Write it down:

This book offers practical tools for working with anxiety, and I encourage you to try at least one exercise in each chapter. Not because they'll eliminate anxiety completely, but because each small step builds your capacity to live alongside it. Some days will still be hard. The monster might growl louder on Mondays, during thunderstorms, or when the world feels too big and too close. But we'll talk about those days too. About how to sit with the discomfort without drowning in it. About how to keep breathing when breathing feels like the hardest thing in the world.

Chapter One

UNDERSTANDING ANXIETY

I've asked myself more times than is necessary: what exactly is anxiety? The question would come at odd moments-while staring at my ceiling at 3 AM, during a perfectly normal coffee with friends, or in the middle of a supermarket aisle, frozen between two brands of cereal. Each time, the answer felt different. Sometimes, it was a tight knot in my stomach; other times a buzzing in my head that wouldn't quiet down, or a constant urge to move, to do something, anything.

The truth is, that anxiety doesn't fit into neat boxes or simple definitions. It shows up differently for everyone. For my neighbor Mike, it's checking his front door lock seven times before bed. For my sister Sarah, it's rehearsing conversations in her head until every word feels wrong. For me, it was turning small decisions into mammoth tasks, as if choosing the wrong breakfast cereal might somehow derail my entire life.

We often mistake anxiety for weakness, for a flaw in our programming. But it's actually an old survival tool that's gone haywire in our modern world. Like an overprotective friend who means well but sees danger everywhere, it tries to keep us safe by keeping us alert to every possible threat—real or imagined. In this chapter, we'll look at anxiety as a set of patterns we can understand, so that we can better recognize its signals, understand its language, and find ways to work with it rather than against it.

FIGHT OR FLIGHT IN EVERYDAY

The morning before my first big presentation, my body kicked into full survival mode as my hands shook while buttoning my shirt, my stomach twisted into knots, and my mind raced through every possible disaster. Though I faced no physical threat, merely the prospect of speaking to a room of people, my body responded as if fighting for survival.

This fight-or-flight response served our ancestors well when outrunning predators or facing physical dangers, as racing hearts and tensed muscles meant survival. Yet now, this same system activates during work deadlines, in crowded elevators, and before difficult conversations. Bodies interpret modern stress through an ancient lens that can't distinguish between a charging bear and an overflowing inbox.

By learning to recognize this response pattern in our bodies, we can work with it rather than against it, noticing tension rising in our shoulders during meetings or breathing changing as we check emails. These reactions aren't flaws but outdated survival tools that need updating for modern life. While we can't deactivate this system entirely, understanding its patterns helps us create space to breathe and respond differently when it activates unnecessarily.

PHYSICAL SYMPTOMS OF ANXIETY

Bessel van der Kolk, one of the world's leading trauma experts, proved that our bodies physically hold our stress and anxiety, revealing through measurable changes what our minds process during times of distress.

Anxiety sets off a chain of biological responses as our muscles tense to prepare for action while blood flows away from the digestive system toward the limbs, and our breathing shifts to pull in more oxygen—all part of readying the body for a response that modern situations rarely require.

Our evolutionary past also explains these physical responses, where muscle tension once protected us from injury during fights or escapes, but now this same protective system activates unnecessarily when we face traffic jams or work deadlines, leaving our bodies tight and sore without purpose.

When anxiety is chronic, it reshapes our body's baseline functioning; so our digestive system grows sensitive, sleep patterns change, and our immune responses are altered in response to this constant state of alert, not from any inherent weakness but from our body's persistent reaction to perceived threats.

The nervous system interprets all potential danger with the same intensity, whether from an angry email or a physical threat, which explains why we feel drained after difficult meetings or social situations even without physical exertion, creating a cycle where physical sensations trigger more anxious thoughts that lead to further physical reactions-a pattern we can only break by understanding how our bodies respond to anxiety.

Physical Symptoms Checklist

Sometimes we misinterpret certain physical sensations as dangerous when they're actually anxiety showing up in our bodies. A tight chest might feel like a heart problem. Dizziness could seem like something's seriously wrong. But often, these sensations are simply anxiety's physical calling cards.

Take a moment to mark which physical changes you notice when anxiety rises:

Body Temperature Changes:

❏ Cold hands or feet

❏ Hot flashes

❏ Sweating in specific places

Muscle Changes:

❑ Jaw tension

❑ Shoulder or neck tightness

❑ Leg restlessness

❑ Hand tremors

Breathing Changes:

❑ Short breaths

❑ Feeling like you can't get enough air

❑ Throat tightness

Stomach and Digestion:

❑ Loss of appetite

❑ Increased hunger

❑ Nausea

❑ Digestive changes

Sleep Patterns:

❑ Trouble falling asleep

❑ Waking up often

❑ Early morning waking

❑ Vivid dreams

What you'll do is circle the three symptoms that bother you most. Typically, these are your early warning signals; in essence, they are the ones to watch for when anxiety first starts building.

The anxiety log sheet can be used to record each time you experience anxiety during the day. This helps you identify what triggers your anxiety, how it affects your body, and how intense it feels at different times. Over time, these records will show patterns you might not notice otherwise.

HOW TO USE THE LOG SHEET

Each entry needs four pieces of information:

1. Time of Day. Record the exact time when you notice anxiety starting. Be specific: "10:30 AM" not just "morning."

2. What Happened Write down three simple facts:
   - ❑ The place you're in
   - ❑ What you're doing
   - ❑ Who else is present

3. Body Signals. Note any changes in how your body feels. Be specific about where and what:
   - ❑ Head: pressure, pain
   - ❑ Chest: breathing changes
   - ❑ Stomach: nausea, tightness
   - ❑ Muscles: tension, trembling

4. Intensity Level Rate how strong the anxiety feels from 1 to 10:
   - ❑ 1: Barely noticeable
   - ❑ 5: Distracting but manageable
   - ❑ 10: Overwhelming

EXAMPLE OF A COMPLETE ENTRY:

TIME	10:30 AM
WHAT HAPPENED	I was giving a presentation in the office meeting room with my whole team present.
BODY SIGNALS	Pressure in head, tight chest, shaky hands
INTENSITY	7

Fill this out for one week and ensure that you make at least three entries each day. Write them as soon as possible after anxiety occurs.

TIME	
WHAT HAPPENED	
BODY SIGNALS	
INTENSITY	

TIME	
WHAT HAPPENED	
BODY SIGNALS	
INTENSITY	

TIME

WHAT HAPPENED

BODY SIGNALS

INTENSITY

TIME

WHAT HAPPENED

BODY SIGNALS

INTENSITY

TIME

WHAT HAPPENED

BODY SIGNALS

INTENSITY

TIME

WHAT HAPPENED

BODY SIGNALS

INTENSITY

Exercise: Mapping Your Anxiety Patterns

We all have things that trigger our anxiety. In my case, I'd say it's plans changing unexpectedly. A friend cancels lunch last minute. A meeting gets moved up by two hours. My child school calls for early pickup. All of these are situations and scenarios that make me feel as if the whole world beneath my feet has shifted. It might be different for you; it might be walking into a room full of strangers, or seeing your phone light up with your boss's name. Or hearing "we need to talk" from someone you love. These are all triggers shaped by our experiences, our fears, and our past, and this exercise, will teach you to see them clearly:

1. Grab a blank page. Any paper will do and doesn't need to be fancy.

2. Start with what you know. Write down three situations that reliably spark your anxiety. Be specific:

   ❑ Not just "social situations" but "walking into a party alone"

   ❑ Not just "work stress" but "speaking up in team meetings"

   ❑ Not just "money worries" but "checking my bank balance"

3. For each situation, note:

   ❑ Where you feel it in your body (tight chest? churning stomach?)

   ❑ What you usually do in response (check your phone? make lists?)

   ❑ What thoughts loop in your head ("I'll mess this up" or "Everyone will notice")

4. Look for patterns:

- ❏ Time of day-Morning anxiety feels different from 3 AM thoughts
- ❏ Places-Home might feel safe while grocery stores set you off
- ❏ People-Some relationships might need more recovery time than others

Tracking Physical and Emotional Responses: Weekly Log

When you are able to recognize the physical sensations and emotional fluctuations that accompany anxiety, you develop greater self-awareness and resilience. Use this tracker to systematically map your daily experiences, providing a comprehensive overview of your emotional landscape and physiological responses.

Day 1

Physical Sensations:

Location of tension: _____

Quality of breath: _____

Energy level: _____

Most noticeable sensation:_____

Emotional State:

Primary emotions: _____

Intensity (1-10): _____

Triggers: _____

What helped: _____

Day 2

Physical Sensations:

Location of tension: _____

Quality of breath: _____

Energy level: _____

Most noticeable sensation: _____

Emotional State:

Primary emotions: _____

Intensity (1-10): _____

Triggers: _____

What helped: _____

Day 3

Physical Sensations:

Location of tension: _____

Quality of breath: _____

Energy level: _____

Most noticeable sensation: _____

Emotional State:

Primary emotions: _____

Intensity (1-10): _____

Triggers: _____

What helped: _____

Day 4

Physical Sensations:

Location of tension: _____

Quality of breath: _____

Energy level: _____

Most noticeable sensation: _____

Emotional State:

Primary emotions: _____

Intensity (1-10): _____

Triggers: _____

What helped: _____

Day 5

Physical Sensations:

Location of tension: _____

Quality of breath: _____

Energy level: _____

Most noticeable sensation: _____

Emotional State:

Primary emotions: _____

Intensity (1-10): _____

Triggers: _____

What helped: _____

Day 6

Physical Sensations:

Location of tension: _____

Quality of breath: _____

Energy level: _____

Most noticeable sensation: _____

Emotional State:

Primary emotions: _____

Intensity (1-10): _____

Triggers: _____

What helped: _____

Day 7

Physical Sensations:

Location of tension: _____

Quality of breath: _____

Energy level: _____

Most noticeable sensation: _____

Emotional State:

Primary emotions: _____

Intensity (1-10): _____

Triggers: _____

What helped: _____

Weekly Reflection

Most common physical response: _____

Recurring emotional pattern: _____

Situations that impacted both: _____

What you learned about your response patterns: _____

_____

_____

Tools that helped most: _____

_____

Look for patterns in how your body and emotions respond to different situations. These patterns help you understand your needs and respond more effectively.

All of this is noticing work; learning to connect the dots that you might have missed before. And your map might surprise you as you work through it because patterns often hide in plain sight until we take time to look for them.

It takes a fair amount of time to adjust to a new environment, a new habit, a new way of seeing things. The same goes for understanding our anxiety. The physical symptoms, the triggers, and the patterns won't make sense overnight. There's no issue in that because you don't need to figure it all out at once.

What matters is that you've started paying attention. You've begun to notice how anxiety shows up in your body, when it tends to appear, and what makes it louder or quieter. This awareness isn't about controlling anxiety or making it disappear. It's about getting to know it, like learning the rhythms of a new place you've moved to.

Some days will be harder than others. You might fill out your anxiety log and notice the same triggers coming up again and again. You might feel frustrated when physical symptoms show up at inconvenient times. This is normal. Understanding anxiety isn't a straight line from confusion to clear—it's more like learning a new language, where some days the words flow and others they stick in your throat.

Take what you've learned in this chapter and hold it lightly. Use the tools when they help, and adapt them when they don't. The goal isn't perfection. It's simply to know yourself a little better than you did before. Let's go and learn a little more about how you can defuse your anxious thoughts.

Chapter Two

DEFUSING ANXIOUS THOUGHTS

I was a "go to summer camp" for the holidays kind of kid and for the most part, it was quite satisfactory and enjoyable. Except for one thing—the high ropes course. Every year, they'd tell us it would build confidence, teach teamwork, and help us overcome fears. But standing forty feet up, clipped to a wire, my mind would flood with thoughts so convincing, so urgent, that my body would freeze completely.

That summer taught me something about anxiety that no textbook could explain. While other kids moved across the ropes with various degrees of nervousness, I discovered my mind had its own special way of turning possibilities into certainties. "The wire might break" became "The wire will break." "I might fall" turned into vivid scenes of falling. Each thought felt more real than the safety harness securing me.

The anxious mind applies this same logic to presentations, health concerns, and social situations-treating each "maybe" as a definite outcome, each possibility as a prediction. But seeing these patterns clearly, recognizing how anxiety writes its own stories, gives us a way to respond differently.

CATCHING YOUR ANXIETY MID-SCENE

There's an analogy that my grandmother loved to use, something about soup and boiling pots, or was it actually about tea kettles? She'd say you can catch water before it boils if you pay attention to the small bubbles forming at the bottom. But wait too long, and suddenly the whole pot is bubbling over.

Catching anxiety works the same way. By the time your heart races and thoughts spin, anxiety has reached full boil. But there are always early signals—small bubbles forming at the bottom of the pot. A slight tension in your jaw during meetings. The urge to check your phone repeatedly while waiting. A flutter in your stomach before social events.

When you learn to read these early signals, you gift yourself the power choice. Before anxiety commands all your attention, before it convinces you that everything is urgent, you have space to respond thoughtfully. Your body offers these quiet warnings-a change in breathing, a shift in posture, a moment of restlessness.

Immediate Action Steps

You want to start with your body since it responds quicker than your mind. The instant you notice anxiety's first signal, which is before analyzing or questioning it, make one deliberate physical change. If you're sitting at your desk when anxiety appears, stand up and walk to a window. If you're entering a social situation, find a quiet corner and feel your feet firmly on the ground. If you're in a meeting, press your hands together under the table.

Next, direct your attention outward instead of inward. Anxiety pulls focus inside to worries and sensations. Break this pattern by noticing three specific things in your environment. Not just glancing around, but really seeing details-the pattern on someone's shirt, the texture of the wall, the play of light through a window. This external focus helps prevent anxiety's inward spiral.

Then adjust your breathing pattern, but not in obvious ways that might increase self-consciousness. Instead of deep breaths that others might notice, take slightly longer exhales while continuing your normal activity. Let each exhale last one count longer than usual. This subtle change helps calm your nervous system without drawing attention.

These steps work best when practiced regularly in calm moments so they become automatic when anxiety first appears. The goal isn't eliminating anxiety but catching it early enough to choose how you'll respond.

LOCATION-SPECIFIC TOOLS

Different situations require different approaches, or as a former meditation teacher used to say: "You cannot use the same key for every lock." Anxiety in a meeting feels different from anxiety at a social event. The tools that help you stay grounded during decision-making might not work in spaces that trigger physical panic.

In Meetings and Presentations

Professional settings require much more subtle approaches. Before the meeting starts, choose your seat strategically; near an exit if you need to step out, or close to a window for a sense of space. Arrive five minutes early to settle into your space and establish a physical anchor point.

During the meeting, you can use micro-movements that others won't notice. Roll your ankles slowly under the table. Press your back firmly against your chair. If anxiety spikes when speaking, pause to take a sip of water-this creates a natural break while helping you reconnect with physical sensation.

Practice this sequence when anxiety rises:

❏ Notice three points of physical contact (feet on floor, back on chair, hands on table)

❏ Focus on one external detail (someone's voice, a color in the room)

❏ Continue your activity while maintaining awareness of these anchors

For presentations, prepare specific points in your talk where you'll briefly reconnect with these anchors. Mark them in your notes as simple dots or stars-small reminders to ground yourself throughout your presentation.

During Social Interactions

At an early career function, watching others interact revealed a key insight about social anxiety-the most engaged people weren't focused on themselves but were fully present with others.

This shifts how we approach social situations. Instead of managing anxiety, practice genuine interest in others. The strategy transforms the experience:

❑ **Set Clear Intentions:** Not "be the life of the party" but "have one genuine conversation." The focus shifts from performance to connection.

❑ **External Focus:** When self-conscious:

  1. Choose one person to talk with

  2. Notice three specific things about them

  3. Let their presence anchor your attention

❑ **Stay in the Flow:** If anxiety rises during a conversation, ask about something they've mentioned. Their response provides natural focus points beyond your thoughts, keeping the interaction genuine while giving you space to reset.

This approach works because it moves attention from internal worry to external connection, making space for real engagement.

While Making Decisions

When anxiety complicates decisions, try this structured approach:

Get Clear

Write down the actual choice: "Should I take this job?" or "Do I want to move?" Just the core decision, not all possible outcomes.

Separate Facts from Stories

Create two columns:

"What I Know"

❏ Concrete facts (salary, location)
❏ Actual requirements
❏ Current circumstances

"What I'm Creating"

❏ Imagined scenarios
❏ Future worries
❏ "What if" stories

Set Boundaries

Give yourself:
❏ Research Deadline: _____
❏ Decision date: _____

This framework helps cut through anxiety's tendency to overcomplicate choices by separating real factors from imagined scenarios.

In Triggering Spaces

Earlier in the book, we talked about triggers, what they are, and where they come from. But some spaces create such immediate and intense anxiety responses that they need their own specific approach. In these situations, this is what I want you to:

Map Your Triggers

Space: _____

Specific trigger points:

1. _____

2. _____

3. _____

Track Your Response

Anxiety level (1-10):

Body sensations at each level:

4: _____

6: _____

8: _____

Create Anchor Points

Identify focusing objects/landmarks:

In this space:_____

Where to look: _____

What to focus on: _____

Remember: The goal isn't to eliminate anxiety but to understand and work with your specific responses in these spaces.

Notes on what helped:

_____

_____

BUILDING RESILIENCE

Resilience is our ability to be with the good stuff as much as the difficult stuff, to bend without breaking when life tests us. Not just surviving challenges, but learning how to carry them differently each time they appear. With anxiety, resilience means developing a relationship with our fears that don't control our choices. Here's what you can do:

Regular Exposure

Building resilience with anxiety requires consistent, deliberate practice. Think of how athletes train-not by immediately tackling their hardest challenges, but by gradually building strength and skill. Start with situations that create mild anxiety but feel manageable.

Create specific opportunities for practice. If speaking up in meetings makes you anxious, begin by making one small comment in low-stakes situations. Notice what happens in your body, how the anxiety moves through you, and what helps you stay present. Each time you practice, you build evidence of your ability to handle discomfort.

Keep track of these practices. Note what worked and what didn't. Maybe morning meetings feel easier than afternoon ones. Maybe certain topics feel more manageable than others. This information helps you build a personalized approach to working with anxiety.

Schedule these into your week and keep a log of what you notice each time—what worked, what didn't, and how your responses changed with practice. This isn't about getting rid of anxiety but about building evidence that you can handle it.

Recovery Training Most people focus only on handling anxiety in the moment, but recovery matters just as much. After anxiety spikes, your nervous system needs reset time. This isn't weakness-it's smart biology. Your body and mind need specific ways to return to baseline.

Create your personal recovery sequence. Some people need physical movement first—a walk around the block, stretching, or deep breathing. Others need mental space through reading, music, or quiet time. Still others process best by talking with someone who understands. Experiment to find what works for you.

Building Support Systems

Anxiety is most overwhelming when we carry it alone. Having reliable support doesn't mean being dependent-it means being smart about how humans actually cope with challenges. Think about the different types of support you need. Some people help you think clearly when anxiety clouds your mind. Others know how to listen without trying to fix everything. Some offer practical help or simply a quiet presence.

Be specific with these people about what helps. Clear communication prevents the frustration of well-meaning but unhelpful support. Let them know if you just need them to listen, or if you want practical suggestions, or if you need help with specific tasks.

Anxiety moves through you like weather; sometimes it is as gentle as rain, other times as fierce as storms. The tools in this chapter help you navigate both kinds of weather. From catching anxiety's early signals to handling specific situations like meetings, social events, and decision-making, you now have practical ways to respond when anxiety rises.

These tools work best when practiced regularly, not just during difficult moments. Like any skill, working with anxiety gets easier with consistent practice and patience. You're not trying to eliminate anxiety but learning to move through life with more confidence, even when anxiety shows up.

Keep building your resilience through small steps forward. Each time you use a tool, each moment you choose to respond differently to anxiety, you strengthen your ability to handle whatever weather comes your way.

In the next chapter, I'm going to teach you how your fear isn't something to be afraid of, but rather something you can work alongside.

Chapter Three
RADICAL ACCEPTANCE OF FEAR

I am scared to say it and let it sink in... and then after a while, tell me how it feels to be that honest with yourself. Notice what happens in your body when you acknowledge fear without trying to fix it or push it away. Notice if your shoulders drop slightly, if your breath deepens, if something inside relaxes just a bit.

Most of us spend enormous energy trying not to feel afraid. We analyze and plan to prevent fear. We avoid situations that might trigger it. We fight against fear when it appears. But this constant battle with fear often causes more suffering than fear itself.

Fear shows up in different flavors. Sometimes, it's about physical safety—that racing heart when walking alone at night. Sometimes, it's social-the stomach flips before giving a presentation. Sometimes it's deeper—the existential fear of uncertainty or the core fear of not being enough. Each type of fear needs its own kind of acceptance.

This chapter explores how to make room for fear without being ruled by it. Not through eliminating fear; that's neither possible nor desirable-but through changing our relationship with it entirely.

TYPES OF FEARS

There are different types of fears; fears that all serve different purposes and show up in different ways in our lives. Knowing which fear is which and how it shows up helps us work with it more effectively.

Survival fears: These emerge from our basic need to stay safe and alive. Your heart races when you hear footsteps behind you at night. Your body tenses when a car swerves too close on the highway. Your muscles prepare to run when you sense danger. These fears trigger immediate physical responses—increased heart rate, shallow breathing, and heightened alertness.

Social fears: These revolve around our need for connection and acceptance. Fear of public speaking makes your voice shake. Fear of rejection keeps you from reaching out to others. Fear of judgment stops you from sharing your ideas. These fears often create physical symptoms like blushing, sweating, or trembling, along with intense self-consciousness.

Existential fears: These touch our deepest questions about life and meaning. Fear of uncertainty about the future. Fear of making the wrong life choices. Fear of living without purpose. These fears often feel heavy and persistent, showing up as a constant background anxiety or periods of intense questioning.

Identity fears: these are the kinds of fears that challenge our sense of self and worth; it's the fear of not being good enough; the fear of failure; the fear of being exposed as inadequate. These fears affect how we see ourselves and often limit our actions and choices. They might keep you from pursuing opportunities, speaking up, or taking risks.

When we work through each of these dears, we'll need to use a different approach. Survival fears need immediate physical calming. Social fears benefit from gradual exposure and practice. Existential fears require exploration and meaning-making. Identity fears need compassionate self-examination.

HOW WE FIGHT FEAR

Our attempts to avoid fear often backfire. We overanalyze to prevent surprises, avoid triggers, and create detailed plans for control. These strategies promise safety but fuel more anxiety.

Avoidance has hidden costs. Skipping presentations, declining invitations, and staying in outgrown situations provide temporary relief but reinforce fear's power. Meanwhile, constant vigilance drains energy that could fuel growth and creativity. Society's messages about fear being weakness add shame to our natural responses.

The pattern is clear:

❑ Feel fear

❑ Judge yourself for feeling it

❑ Try to suppress or avoid it

❑ Experience intensified anxiety

❑ Increase avoidance

Notice your resistance patterns:

❑ Endless analysis and planning

❑ Avoiding challenges

❑ Seeking perfect certainty

❑ Constant self-monitoring

Fear remains part of being human, but you choose how to respond. Instead of fighting it, learn to carry fear differently. Make space for it without letting it make your decisions. Move toward what matters, even when fear joins the journey.

The "It's Okay" Practice

Start with something that creates mild anxiety-not your biggest fear, but one that creates noticeable discomfort. Notice where this fear lives in your body. Say out loud: "It's okay that I feel afraid right now." Notice what happens when you grant this permission. Add specifics: "It's okay that my heart is racing. It's okay that my thoughts are spinning. It's okay to feel uncertain."

Fear Relationship Exercise

Take out your journal and write about one specific fear. Detail exactly how you've tried to fight it in the past—the avoidance, the analysis, the attempts at control. Then write how this fear might actually be trying to protect you. What is it warning you about? What does it want you to know?

Daily Fear Check-in

Each morning, rate your fear level from 1-10. Instead of trying to lower this number, get curious about it. What's contributing to today's number? How does this fear feel in your body? Where do you notice it most? Write down your observations without trying to change anything.

Fear Exposure Log

Keep a weekly record of situations that trigger fear. Note:

❑ What happened
❑ Your initial fear response
❑ What you did next
❑ What you learned

This isn't about judging your responses but about building awareness of your patterns with fear.

Weekly Fear Review

Set aside time each week to review your experiences with fear. Notice what situations consistently trigger fear, how your responses have changed, and what new patterns emerge. Look for small wins-moments when you carried fear differently or moved forward despite it.

Remember: These exercises aim to change your relationship with fear, not eliminate it. Practice them regularly, starting with smaller fears and gradually working with more challenging ones.

The 5-4-3-2-1 Technique

When fear or anxiety takes hold, your nervous system needs clear signals to remember you're safe. Grounding works by engaging your senses purposefully, pulling your attention from racing thoughts back to present-moment experiences. Like dropping an anchor in stormy waters, sensory awareness helps steady your mind when it feels adrift.

This simple but powerful exercise guides you through your senses systematically. Each step helps your brain shift from threat response to present awareness.

Notice:

❑ 5 things you can SEE: Look around slowly, noting colors, shapes, and details

❑ 4 things you can FEEL: Focus on physical sensations-the texture of clothing, air on the skin

❑ 3 things you can HEAR: Listen for both close and distant sounds

❑ 2 things you can SMELL: Notice any scents in your environment

❑ 1 thing you can TASTE: Observe the current taste in your mouth

Practice this whenever anxiety rises or thoughts start racing. The order matters less than the act of moving through your senses deliberately. Write your observations here:

See:

Feel:

Hear:

Smell:

Taste:

What changed after completing this exercise? Is there anything that you noticed before and after grounding?

A note to remember: Grounding works best when practiced regularly, not just during intense moments.

Some things that I want you to remember (especially about your fear) are the following: that just because you feel fear, it necessarily means that something bad will happen. Your fear speaks loudly but often tells stories about futures that never arrive, dangers that exist only in imagination, and disasters that live only in worried thoughts.

Your relationship with fear will change as you practice these tools. Each time you make space for fear without letting it control your choices, you build evidence of your capacity to handle uncertainty. Each time you move toward what matters despite anxiety, you strengthen your ability to carry fear differently.

Fear will show up throughout your life when you pursue meaningful goals, build important relationships, or face new challenges. Let it come along for the ride. Let it remind you what matters enough to feel scared about. Let it point toward what you care about deeply enough to feel afraid of losing. Your fear, in its own way, highlights your values, your connections, and your aspirations. Welcome it as a sign that you're living fully, growing consistently, and staying engaged with what gives your life meaning. Let's move on to the next chapter and continue the work of building our fear response kit.

Chapter Four

BUILDING YOUR FEAR RESPONSE TOOLKIT

Someone once told me something about resources. And not resources such as money, shelter, food. No. Those are good though. They were talking about internal resources, about building a well inside yourself that you can draw from when fear makes everything feel scarce.

Fear has its own rhythm in each person's life. It pulses through a morning presentation, echoes in quiet moments of doubt, and rises in crowded spaces. Your body knows this rhythm. Your mind carries its particular melodies. The way your hands shake slightly before speaking up. The tightness in your throat when entering a room full of strangers. The racing thoughts that come at 3 AM.

Generic solutions fall short because fear isn't generic. It lives in your specific memories, your unique experiences, and your personal patterns. A toolkit for working with fear must grow from this understanding-not from collecting techniques, but from knowing exactly what you need in your hardest moments.

RECOVERY AND RESET

Rest is anything that makes you feel safe enough to be, and by being, I mean safe enough to be present in your body again after fear has moved through it. Safe enough to feel your breath settle, to let your shoulders drop, to allow your mind to expand beyond survival mode.

After fear floods your system, your body and mind need specific ways to return to steady ground. Some bodies ask for movement; that is walking, stretching, and dancing fear out of tight muscles. Some minds need quiet like a dark room, soft music, and time to process what happened. Some hearts need a connection, a friend's voice, a hand to hold, a simple presence. The moments after fear matter as much as how you handle fear itself. They create a bridge between surviving and learning, between enduring and growing. Each time you recover from fear, you build evidence of your capacity to handle it.

Let me show you how to develop recovery practices that match your personal needs and practices that help you find your way back to solid ground after fear shakes it.

Types of Rest

There are many types of rest and each of these cater to different parts of ourselves that fear affects. After fear moves through your system, your body and mind signal specific needs for restoration. Understanding these different types of rest helps you respond more precisely to what your system asks for.

Psychological Rest

Your mind processes thousands of thoughts daily, but fear amplifies this mental activity exponentially. Every possibility becomes a potential threat. Every scenario needs analysis. Every moment demands vigilance. This psychological hyperactivity exhausts your brain's resources, similar to how running a computer with too many programs eventually overheats the system.

After intense fear or anxiety, your mind needs specific forms of psychological rest. This means more than just "not thinking." It requires active permission to release responsibility, to stop problem-solving, and to cease constant threat assessment. This type of rest allows your mind to return to its natural rhythm rather than maintaining high alert.

Physical Rest

The body works overtime when it is operating from a state of fear. Your muscles tense to prepare for action. Your heart rate increases to pump more blood to major muscle groups. Your breathing becomes shallow to prepare for quick movement. Even after fear subsides, these physical changes can persist, leaving your body in a state of preparation for danger that never comes. Physical rest after fear means helping your body return to its baseline state. This involves more than just lying down. Physical rest, in essence, gives clear signals to your body that the danger has passed, and that it can finally release its defensive postures.

Post-Fear Rest Practice: An Exercise

After intense fear, your system needs specific types of care—like a garden needs different kinds of nourishment after a storm. This practice guides you through restoring different parts of yourself that fear affects. Each element addresses a particular way your system responds to fear, helping you recover more fully than just waiting for fear to fade.

This sequence combines physical, sensory, psychological, and creative rest into one restorative practice. Think of it as a map for recovery, showing you how to tend to each part of yourself that fear has taxed.

Choose a quiet hour when you won't be interrupted. Gather what you'll need: comfortable clothes, a soft blanket, perhaps a journal. This practice combines different types of rest to help your system fully recover after fear.

Start with Physical Rest (15 minutes): Lie down somewhere comfortable. Place one hand on your chest, and one on your belly. Let your body settle into stillness. Notice any areas that still hold tension from fear. Give these areas permission to soften.

Move to Sensory Rest (10 minutes): Dim the lights or close your eyes. Remove any constricting clothing. Create as much quiet as possible. If complete silence feels uncomfortable, play soft instrumental music. Let your senses dial down their alertness.

Create Psychological Rest (15 minutes): Instead of trying to empty your mind, give it something simple to focus on. Watch your breath and move your hands on your chest and belly. When thoughts about what scared you arise, notice them without following their stories.

End with Creative Rest (10 minutes): Look at something beautiful-artwork, nature photographs, or out a window. Let your mind wander without purpose. Notice how your perspective naturally expands beyond fear's narrow focus.

Pay attention to which type of rest your system responds to most strongly. Some people need more physical rest, others more sensory quiet. Let your experience guide how you adjust these times and approaches.

LEARNING TO TRUST YOURSELF AGAIN

Fear is a natural part of growth because it signals that you're stretching beyond your comfort zone. Like muscles that must break down to grow stronger, your comfort zone needs to expand through experiences that initially feel uncertain. The discomfort doesn't mean you're doing something wrong, it often means you're growing in exactly the right direction.

When we avoid this natural fear, we stagnate. Think of a plant reaching toward sunlight-it must push through the soil, face wind and rain, and risk exposure to grow taller. Our growth follows similar patterns. Starting a new job, deepening relationships, and pursuing goals. These important steps forward naturally bring fear because they ask us to become more than we currently are.

Understanding fear as a growth signal changes how we carry it. Instead of seeing fear as a warning to stop, we can view it as evidence we're expanding. This doesn't make fear comfortable, but it makes it meaningful-a natural companion on the path toward what matters most.

Three Foundations of Self-Trust

I know that it might not feel like you are capable of trusting yourself right now, especially when fear has eroded that trust over time. Each time fear makes a decision feel impossible, or anxiety convinces you to doubt your judgment, this trust weakens further. Building trust in yourself works like strengthening any foundation, you first need an understanding of the core elements that support it.

Let me show you the three foundations that create lasting self-trust. Each one builds upon the other, to create a base strong enough to withstand fear's storms.

❑ **Trust Your Decision-Making.** Your mind holds wisdom even when doubt clouds it. Notice the small choices you make daily—what to eat, when to rest, who to see. Each decision, whether it worked out or taught a lesson, builds evidence of your capability to choose wisely.

❑ **Trust Life's Unfolding.** Life rarely follows our plans, yet unexpected turns often lead to meaningful growth. Think of chance meetings that became important relationships or apparent setbacks that opened new paths. Possibilities exist beyond fear's narrow view.

❑ **Trust Your Resilience.** Every obstacle faced and fear moved through proves your strength. Remember times you thought you couldn't handle something but found a way. You've grown through difficulties and discovered capabilities you didn't know you had.

Building Trust Practice

Fear often creates a gap between what you can handle and what you believe you can handle. This practice helps close that gap by showing you concrete evidence of your own capabilities. Think of it as creating a map of your existing strengths while exploring a new territory of self-trust.

Many of us look outside ourselves for validation, we gather opinions like we do jewlery and want absolute certainty before making our moves. This exercise turns your attention inward so that you can recognize and strengthen your own inner guidance system. We will work with small decisions first, then gradually expand to bigger ones, so that you are able to build trust the same way you build any skill, through consistent practice and careful attention to what works.

Throughout all of it, we're going to find the balance between healthy caution and paralyzing doubt, between wisdom and fear. You will learn how to distinguish between fear's voice and your own knowing.

First things first, take an hour where you won't be interrupted. Bring a journal, something to drink, and a willingness to explore your relationship with trust. Let me guide you through this practice step by step.

Start with Small Decisions

Do you have a small decision that you need to make today? What is the first instinct about what feels right? Write down this initial response before doubt or analysis begins. Then track what happens when you follow this instinct rather than overthinking. Practice this with small choices first—what to eat, when to rest, and how to spend an hour of free time.

Map Your History of Handling Challenges

Write down three difficulties you've faced and moved through. For each one, note:

❑ What helped you get through it

❑ What you learned about yourself

❑ How it changed you

❑ What strengths it revealed

Notice where you already trust yourself. Maybe you trust your ability to learn new skills, or your judgment about people, or your capacity to handle certain types of situations. Build from this existing foundation.

Create Evidence of Trust

Collect proof of your ability to trust yourself. Each time you make a decision that works out, write it down. When you handle a challenge well, record it. As you move through uncertainty and find your way, note it. This builds a personal reference library of your capability.

Practice trusting your body's signals, your heart's knowing, your mind's wisdom. Start with what feels manageable and gradually expand from there.

"It's Okay" Acceptance Practice

It's okay to be uncertain about big decisions, to worry about change unfolding in your life, and to feel nervous around new people even when you want to connect. It's okay to feel unsure of your path forward or to learn as you go instead of having everything figured out. These natural fears signal growth, not weakness.

When we fight against our fears and uncertainties, we create more tension and resistance. This exercise helps you practice accepting your natural human responses, making space for both caution and courage. By acknowledging what's okay, you begin to loosen fear's grip and find more room to move forward.

Take a moment now to explore what feels okay in your own experience:

Fill in your own:

When I face challenges, it's okay to: _____

When making decisions, it's okay to: _____

In relationships, it's okay to: _____

With my goals, it's okay to: _____

About my fears, it's okay to: _____

Now write your personal "It's okay" statements:

Right now, it's okay that I: _____

With this specific fear, it's okay to: _____

Moving forward, it's okay if I: _____

Take a moment to notice how accepting these fears, rather than fighting them, creates space for both caution and courage. What shifts when you allow both to exist?

What I notice when I accept my fears: _____

Where I feel more space to move: _____

What becomes possible: _____

Accepting fear doesn't mean letting it decide for you-it means making room for growth alongside uncertainty.

What I have learned throughout my life, which is what we'll get into a little more in the next chapter, is that the more I try to ignore something, the louder, and more persistent it gets. Fear works this way too. The more we try to push it away, fight against it, and pretend it doesn't exist, the stronger its hold becomes. Fear will, without a doubt still appear when you pursue meaningful goals, build important relationships, and face new challenges, but what I want you to remember is that it will always point you toward what matters to you. It shows up because you care, and because you're engaged with life, because you're growing beyond what feels comfortable. Let it remind you what you value enough to feel afraid about. Let it guide you toward what needs your attention and care. Most importantly, let it show you your own strength, not in fearlessness, but in your willingness to move forward even when fear joins you for the journey.

Chapter Five

BUILDING COURAGE

One of my favorite things to do is to ask people what they think courage is or how they would define it. Over the years I've collected a lot of interesting responses and a few of my favorites are:

A six-year-old who said courage is "doing something even when your tummy feels funny about it." A firefighter who described it as "being scared but showing up anyway." A grandmother who said courage is "choosing love over fear, every single time."

These definitions share something important—none of them mention fearlessness. Real courage lives in that space between fear and action, in those moments when something matters enough to move through fear rather than avoid it. Not because the fear disappears, but because you've learned to carry it differently.

This chapter explores how courage grows through practice, through small choices that build evidence of your capability, and through discovering what becomes possible when fear no longer makes your decisions.

TYPES OF COURAGE

When reflecting on past experiences, I realized I had acted more bravely than I initially thought. While courage might seem straightforward-acting despite fear—closer examination reveals its complexity across different situations. Sometimes courage meant sitting with painful emotions when instinct urged escape.

Other times, it emerged as speaking truth when silence felt safer, or confronting physical discomfort. Understanding these types of courage helps us recognize our own bravery and identify areas for growth.

❑ **Emotional Courage:** Most people try to escape uncomfortable feelings, but emotional courage means staying present with our full range of emotions. It involves sitting with sadness without trying to fix it, facing anxiety without running from it, and acknowledging anger without acting on it. This type of courage grows when we allow ourselves to feel vulnerable, grieve losses fully, and experience joy deeply even when such happiness feels frightening.

❑ **Social Courage:** Being genuinely yourself around others often requires more bravery than facing physical challenges. Social courage manifests as expressing true thoughts even when they differ from the group, setting boundaries despite pushback, and showing up authentically when it feels safer to wear a mask. It means risking rejection for real connection and speaking your truth even with a shaking voice.

❑ **Physical Courage:** While often associated with extreme sports or heroic rescues, physical courage appears more frequently in daily moments of discomfort. It emerges when we stay with frightening physical sensations, attempt something despite possible failure, or face scary medical procedures. This courage builds through small steps of facing bodily discomfort while maintaining presence.

❑ **Moral Courage:** Standing for your values when it costs you something requires its own kind of bravery. Moral courage surfaces when speaking up against injustice while others remain silent, choosing integrity over convenience, and following conscience down difficult paths. Though this courage often feels lonely, it connects us deeply with what matters most.

Exploring Different Types of Courage-Reflection Worksheet

After reading about the four types of courage, take time to reflect on your own experiences and growth areas.

When was a time you showed emotional courage by staying with difficult feelings? What helped you do this?

In what situation could you practice more social courage? What's one small step you could take?

Describe a moment when you demonstrated physical courage. How did it feel in your body?

What's a value worth standing up for? What's one way you could show moral courage in supporting it?

Looking at all four types of courage, which area would you like to develop most? Why?

THE VALUES AND ANXIETY MATRIX

The Values-Anxiety Matrix shows how values guide action even when fear rises. Think of it as two intersecting forces: what matters to you (values) and what scares you (anxiety). Where these meet, you find opportunities for meaningful action.

When you value growth, anxiety about new challenges points toward learning opportunities. Your fear of speaking up in meetings highlights your chances to contribute. When you value connection, social anxiety reveals places to build authentic relationships.

Instead of trying to eliminate fear, use your values as a compass. They help you choose which anxious moments are worth moving through. This creates purpose-driven courage rather than action based on "shoulds" or pressure to overcome fear.

For example: Growth value meets job interview anxiety: Prepare thoroughly, show up fully Connection value meets social anxiety: Ask one genuine question, listen deeply Learning value meets fear of failure: Take one small step, focus on progress.

This matrix transforms fear from a stop sign into a signpost toward what matters.

Values & Anxiety Reflection Worksheet

Looking at your values, which one feels most important right now? What anxiety shows up when you try to live it?

When anxiety arises, how could your values help guide your next step?

Identify a current challenge. What value is it pointing toward? What small action could you take?

Which of your values feels hardest to act on because of fear? What's at stake?

Think of a time your values helped you move through anxiety. What did you learn?

MAINTAINING COURAGE

You won't always feel brave or courageous or feel that you have it in you to face what scares you. I know because I've spent entire weeks hiding from phone calls, whole months playing it safe, and seasons of my life where fear made more decisions than courage.

But here's what I've learned about maintaining courage: it works like a garden rather than a fortress. You don't build it once and expect it to last forever. Instead, you tend it daily through small actions, protect it during storms, and strengthen it through consistent care.

Courage needs specific kinds of nourishment to stay strong. It needs people who remind you of your capacity for bravery when you forget. It needs practices that build evidence of your capability. Most importantly, it needs patience during times when fear feels stronger than your ability to face it.

Let me show you how to maintain courage in ways that last.

Handling Setbacks

Document the setback thoroughly-what happened externally and internally? Note when anxiety took over, when fear stopped you, or when uncertainty made you step back. Include both the situation and your response to it.

Create a practical plan for your next attempt. This might mean finding someone to practice with, developing a clearer outline, or learning specific anxiety management strategies. Consider what emotional support you need, whether that's a check-in buddy, a friend to text, or a mentor's guidance.

Make your next attempt manageable by breaking it down. Rather than tackling the whole presentation, start with practicing the opening. Instead of speaking in every meeting, begin with one question. Build your confidence step by step through this sequence.

Set specific dates for action. Mark your practice sessions and the next attempt on your calendar. Don't wait for confidence or motivation – they often follow action rather than lead it. Choose when you'll return to courage, then follow through regardless of how ready you feel.

Building Beyond Setbacks

Use setbacks to identify exactly where fear has useful information for you. When fear of public speaking stops you, it might reveal a need to strengthen your preparation routine. When social anxiety holds you back, it might show you which social skills need practice. Instead of seeing setbacks as failures, treat them as detailed feedback about what needs attention.

Turn each setback into a specific experiment. If a presentation didn't go well, try changing just one element next time-maybe your preparation method, your breathing technique, or your opening lines. Test different approaches until you find what works for you.

Build a 'courage resume', not of perfect victories, but of real attempts. Include the times you stayed in uncomfortable situations instead of leaving, the moments you spoke up even if your voice shook, and the decisions you made despite uncertainty. Each attempt, successful or not, proves you can face fear and take action anyway.

Let each setback shape your next brave choice. Use what you learn to adjust your approach, strengthen your strategies, and choose challenges that stretch you just enough to grow without overwhelming your current capabilities.

Value-Based Decision-Making Worksheet

This worksheet helps you make decisions aligned with your values when fear arises. First, identify a specific value (like honesty, growth, or connection) and a current decision you're facing where fear is holding you back. Write down why this value matters deeply to you and how acting on it could make a difference. Next, get clear about your fear by noting physical sensations and thoughts that arise. Instead of trying to eliminate the fear, design a small, specific action step that moves you toward your value. Note what support you need and set a clear date for action. After taking the step, reflect on what worked and what you learned. Finally, make a clear commitment by filling in the statement at the bottom, linking your chosen action to your core value. This process helps transform abstract values into concrete, courageous action.

Your Value in Focus:

The Situation:

What decision are you facing? _____

What fear is coming up? _____

Create Your Action Plan:

1. Connect to Your Value

❑ What makes this value important to you?

❑ How would acting on it make a difference?

_____

_____

_____

2. Name Your Fear

Physical sensations: _____

Thoughts that arise: _____

What's the worst that could happen? _____

3. Design Your Next Step

Smallest possible action: _____

Support needed: _____

When exactly will you do this? _____

4. Track Your Progress

What worked? _____

What could adjust next time? _____

How did it align with your values? _____

Your Commitment:

I choose to _____ by (date)_____
because my value of _____ matters more than my
fear of _____.

The Values-Based Courage Exercise

Most people wait to feel brave before taking action. They wait
for fear to shrink, for confidence to grow, for the perfect moment
when action feels safe. But courage grows through doing, not
waiting. This exercise helps you take one specific action that
matters, even while feeling afraid.

Take an hour where you won't be interrupted. Bring a pen, paper,
and willingness to explore the intersection between your values
and your fears.

Step One: Choose Your Value

Pick one value that matters deeply to you right now. Not what
you think should matter, but what actually moves you. Maybe
it's authenticity, creativity, connection, or growth.

Step Two: Notice Fear's Role

Look at how fear might stop you from living this value fully. Be
specific. If you value connection, maybe fear of rejection stops
you from reaching out. If you value creativity, perhaps fear of
judgment keeps your ideas hidden.

Step Three: Choose One Action

Select one small action that expresses your chosen value, something that creates just enough discomfort to feel challenging but not overwhelming. Make it specific and doable within the next 24 hours:

❑ A conversation you need to have

❑ An idea you want to share

❑ A boundary you need to set

❑ A new situation to enter

Step Four: Create Your Plan

Decide exactly when and where you'll take this action. The more specific your plan, the more likely you'll follow through. Include what support you need and how you'll handle fear when it shows up.

Building Courage Tracker

Track your journey of facing fears and building resilience. Notice patterns in what helps you move forward and recover effectively.

This Week's Focus

Value I'm expressing: _____

Fear I'm working with: _____

Small action I'll take: _____

MONDAY

Action taken: _____

Fear level (1-10): _____

What helped: _____

_____

Recovery needed: _____

TUESDAY

Action taken: _____

Fear level (1-10): _____

What helped: _____

_____

Recovery needed: _____

WEDNESDAY

Action taken: _____

Fear level (1-10): _____

What helped: _____

_____

Recovery needed: _____

THURSDAY

Action taken: _____

Fear level (1-10): _____

What helped: _____

_____

Recovery needed: _____

FRIDAY

Action taken: _____

Fear level (1-10): _____

What helped: _____

_____

Recovery needed: _____

SATURDAY

Action taken: _____

Fear level (1-10): _____

What helped: _____

_____

Recovery needed: _____

SUNDAY

Action taken: _____

Fear level (1-10): _____

What helped: _____

_____

Recovery needed: _____

WEEKLY LEARNING

Most challenging moment: _____

Most helpful support: _____

Recovery practice that worked: _____

What I learned about my courage: _____

_____

```
PLANNING FORWARD

Next small step: _____

Support I need: _____

Recovery plan: _____.

Value guiding me: _____
```

Remember: Building courage isn't about eliminating fear but about taking meaningful action alongside it. Each attempt strengthens your capacity to move forward.

Some time ago, I read something that sometimes the bravest thing we can do is simply return—return to what scares us, return to what matters, and return to trying even after setbacks. Courage doesn't always roar. Sometimes, it whispers in quiet moments when you choose to face one small fear, take one uncertain step, and try one more time. Your relationship with fear will continue to evolve. Some days, courage will flow easily, other days, fear will feel overwhelming. But you now have tools to work with fear differently, to build courage consistently, and to take meaningful action even when fear joins you for the ride.

Remember this as you close this last page of the chapter: Every time you choose action over avoidance, movement over paralysis, facing fear over running from it, you strengthen your capacity for courage. Not because the fear disappears, but because you've learned to carry it differently.

Conclusion

Courage is about moving with fear rather than being moved by it. Whenever you choose to face what scares you, be it through emotional vulnerability, social authenticity, physical challenge, or moral stance, you strengthen this capacity. Not through grand gestures, but through small, deliberate choices that align with what matters most.

Your relationship with courage will have peaks and valleys. Some days, fear will feel overwhelming, while others will flow with unexpected bravery; what matters isn't the absence of fear, but your willingness to keep showing up, to let your values guide you, and to take one uncertain step after another.

As you move forward, I want you to rest on the reminder that courage grows not because fear disappears, but because you learn to carry it differently. In choosing action over avoidance, in returning to what matters even after setbacks, you aren't just acting courageously; you're becoming more courageous. This capacity lives within you, waiting to be expressed through each brave choice you make.

THE ACT SELF-THERAPY TOOLKIT

A Complete Guide to Lifelong Emotional
Growth and Psychological Flexibility

Introduction

Where in your body do you feel most at home? For some people, it's the steady drum of their heartbeat. For others, it's the rise and fall of their breath. These rhythms—remind us that we already carry deep wisdom within.

Too often we look outside ourselves for answers that already live in our bones, our breath, our beating hearts. While guides and teachers can illuminate the path, your deepest knowing comes from learning to trust your inner compass.

This book emerged from witnessing countless moments of self-discovery-people accessing wisdom they didn't know they had, finding strength they thought was lost, and becoming their own most trusted guide. Where in your life could you listen more deeply to your own knowing? What might change if you trust yourself as much as your heart trusts itself to beat?

As you move through these pages, I invite you to try at least one exercise that calls to you. Let it be an experiment in reconnecting with your inner wisdom. Because just like your heart knows how to keep beating, you know more than you think about how to heal, grow, and thrive.

Chapter One

FOUNDATIONS
OF SELF-THERAPY

I could tell you that self-therapy is never needing help from others, always having the answers within, and being completely self-reliant. But that would be a lie. True self-therapy is something much more nuanced; it means building a relationship with yourself strong enough to know when to rely on your own wisdom and when to seek support from others.

Think of self-therapy as developing a deep friendship with yourself. Just like any important relationship, it requires honesty about your needs, respect for your limits, and understanding of your patterns. Some days this means sitting quietly with difficult feelings until they show you what they need. Other days it means reaching out to a therapist or trusted friend because you recognize when you need more support than you can give yourself.

Many believe self-therapy requires hours of meditation, endless journaling, or constant self-analysis. They think it means never feeling overwhelmed or always knowing exactly what to do. These misconceptions often prevent people from developing practices they can actually sustain. This chapter explores how to build real self-therapy skills; ones that work in the midst of busy lives, emotional challenges, and regular human struggles.

3 PRINCIPLES OF SELF-THERAPY

We often seek perfection when what we really need is progress. True growth embraces both victories and setbacks as essential parts of the journey. Here are three core principles that make self-therapy sustainable, each illustrated with a practical example:

❑ **Empathy:** Our ability to understand and care for our inner experience shapes how we face challenges. When anxiety about a job interview rises, instead of harsh self-judgment, you might say: "Of course, I'm feeling nervous-this matters to me. What support do I need right now?" This response creates space for both acknowledgment and care.

❑ **Authenticity:** Our willingness to be honest with ourselves forms the foundation of real growth. When feeling overwhelmed at work, instead of maintaining a façade, you acknowledge: "I'm struggling to manage my workload. I need to reassess my boundaries and perhaps ask for help." This honesty opens the door to meaningful change.

❑ **Vulnerability:** Our courage to feel full, even when it's uncomfortable, builds true resilience. After a relationship ends, rather than rushing to "move on," you allow yourself to write: "Today hurts. I miss them. I'm scared of being alone. And that's okay to feel." This openness to emotion creates deeper self-understanding.

Together, these principles create a foundation for growth that honors your humanity rather than demanding perfection.

MISCONCEPTIONS ABOUT SELF-THERAPY

There is a lot of things that people misunderstand about self-therapy. Many imagine it means sitting alone analyzing every thought, always knowing the right answers, or never needing support from others. Let me show you these misconceptions and what true self-therapy actually offers.

❑ **Self-Therapy Means Total Independence:** While some think it means handling everything alone, true self-therapy builds discernment about when to work through challenges independently and when to seek support. It actually improves your ability to ask for help by teaching you to read your needs accurately.

❑ **Self-Therapy Requires Hours of Practice:** Many picture-long meditation sessions and extensive journaling. Reality: it integrates into daily life through small moments of awareness and brief check-ins that build over time.

❑ **Self-Therapy Means Always Having Answers:** There's a myth that self-therapy should produce instant clarity and solutions. Instead, it develops your capacity to sit with uncertainty and trust that understanding emerges gradually through experience.

❑ **Self-Therapy Replaces Professional Help:** Rather than replacing professional support, self-therapy enhances it. It helps you bring deeper self-awareness and clearer articulation of needs to your sessions, complementing rather than replacing other forms of support.

BALANCING SELF-RELIANCE AND SEEKING HELP

Finding a balance between independence and seeking help isn't about becoming completely self-reliant or overly dependent. It's about developing wisdom to recognize what each situation needs.

Trust your inner resources when:

❑ Emotions feel manageable (like pre-presentation anxiety)

❑ You need quiet reflection to make decisions

❑ Past experience offers useful guidance

Seek outside perspective when:

❑ Patterns keep repeating despite your efforts

❑ Usual coping strategies aren't enough

❑ Life transitions overwhelm your current resources

Start noticing which challenges resolve through self-reflection and which shift only after getting support. This awareness helps you respond more effectively to each situation, honoring both your capacity for self-healing and your need for connection. The goal isn't independence or dependence, but knowing how to meet yourself exactly where you are.

YOUR PERSONAL HEALING STYLE

Not everyone processes emotions the same way. Some people need movement when feelings get intense—walking, running, dancing their way through anxiety. Others need quiet space to write or reflect. Some process best through conversation, while others find clarity in solitude. Understanding these differences helps you stop fighting your natural tendencies and start working with them instead.

Think about how you naturally handle challenges when no one tells you what to do. In moments of stress, you might automatically reach for the phone to talk it through with someone. Or perhaps you instinctively seek solitude, needing to process internally before sharing with others. Maybe you find yourself unable to think clearly until you've moved your body, or you might need complete stillness to make sense of your feelings.

These natural tendencies offer important clues about your personal healing style. Notice when you feel most capable of handling difficulties. Some people think most clearly early in the morning before the day's demands begin. Others find their strength in the evening hours when the world quiets down. Your energy patterns, natural rhythms, and instinctive responses all shape how you best process emotions and challenges.

Personal Healing Style Worksheet

Take a moment to map out your natural tendencies for processing emotions and handling challenges.

Energy & Timing

When do you feel most clear-headed? _____

What time of day do you process emotions best?_____

How much alone time do you need to recharge? _____

Processing Preferences

How do you naturally handle intense emotions? (Check all that apply.)

❑ Movement (walking, running, dancing)

❑ Quiet reflection

❑ Talking with others

❑ Creative expression

❑ Solitude

❑ Other: _____

Environment

Where do you feel most grounded? _____.

What elements help you feel calm? (light, sound, space) _____.

_____

What conditions make it harder to process? _____.

Support Style

Do you process internally first or do you need to talk it out?

_____

What kind of support helps most in difficult moments?

_____

What type of guidance feels most useful?

_____

Your Patterns

Looking at your answers, what key patterns do you notice about your healing style?

_____

_____

How can you better honor these natural tendencies?

_____

_____

The Activity: Your Recent Challenge Review

Take an hour when you won't be interrupted. Choose a challenge you faced in the last month, something significant enough to remember clearly but not so huge it feels overwhelming to examine. Find a quiet space and gather what helps you think clearly—perhaps a journal, something to drink, or comfortable seating.

First Notice: Explore how this challenge first appeared in your life. What physical sensations signaled something was wrong? Maybe tension in your shoulders, changes in your appetite, or sleep disruption. What thoughts started circling in your mind? How did your emotions shift? Write down everything you remember about these early warning signs.

Pay special attention to what helped you recognize you needed support. Did someone else point out changes in your behavior? Did you notice yourself acting differently? Understanding your personal warning signs helps you catch future challenges earlier.

Natural Response: Examine what you automatically did to handle this challenge. Did you talk to friends? Seek professional help? Try to solve it alone. Write down every coping strategy you used, whether it helped or not. Be specific about what worked and what didn't. If calling a friend helped, what about that conversation made a difference? If meditation didn't work, what got in the way?

This exploration reveals patterns in how you naturally cope with difficulties. Maybe you discover you handle challenges better when you combine social support with alone time for processing. Or perhaps you notice you need physical movement before you can think clearly about problems.

Creating Your Framework:

Use these insights to design an approach that matches your natural style. Think about:

❑ What environment helps you think most clearly? Consider lighting, noise level, temperature, and space.

❑ Which tools actually fit into your daily life? Focus on practices you can sustainably maintain.

❑ What kind of support matches your processing style? This might include professional help, peer support, or specific friends who understand how you work through things.

Build this framework around your natural tendencies rather than fighting against them. If you know you process best through movement, make sure your coping strategies include physical activity. If you think most clearly in the morning, schedule important self-reflection time then.

ACT Challenge Review

Reflect on a recent difficulty using ACT principles. The goal is to understand your patterns and strengthen your ability to respond with flexibility.

The Challenge: What situation did you face?

Initial thoughts and feelings:

Where did you notice it in your body?

Defusion & Acceptance: What stories did your mind tell?

Which feelings did you try to avoid?

Present Moment: What helped you stay grounded?

What pulled you away from the present?

Values & Action: Which values guided you?

What small step did you take?

Learning: What worked well?

What would you do differently?

Remember: Approach this reflection with curiosity rather than judgment. Each challenge builds your psychological flexibility.

So the other day I was thinking about how when I'm unsure about something, I'll quickly text a friend and ask them: "hey, this is the situation... what do you think?" Then I realized that in most instances, when I do that, I'm never really looking for their answer. Deep down, I usually know what feels right. I'm just seeking permission to trust what I already know.

We do this a lot—look outside ourselves for answers we already carry. We ask others to validate our feelings, confirm our decisions, and tell us what we should do next. Sometimes we need this outside perspective. But often, we're just looking for someone to reflect on what we already understand.

Learning to be your own support doesn't mean never reaching out. It means building a relationship with yourself strong enough to recognize when you already know what you need, and when you genuinely need other perspectives. It means trusting that inner voice that whispers the truth, even when fear tries to drown it out.

The tools in this chapter offer ways to strengthen this relationship with yourself. Use them. Practice them. Let them help you remember how much wisdom you already carry. In the next chapter, we'll explore how to integrate them all together.

Chapter Two

THE INTEGRATION PROCESS

There's a difference between knowing something and living it. Between understanding a concept and embodying it. Between having tools and actually using them when you need them most. I see this gap most clearly in my own life-knowing exactly how mindfulness helps with anxiety, yet finding myself holding my breath during difficult moments. Having all the techniques for self-compassion, yet falling into harsh self-criticism when I make mistakes.

This space between knowledge and action isn't about failing or doing something wrong. It's about the natural process of turning new skills into lived experience. Like learning to play an instrument-you can understand music theory perfectly but still need practice before your fingers move naturally across the keys.

The integration process asks for something different than just collecting more knowledge or gathering more tools. It asks you to take what you've learned and work with it until it becomes part of you, until these skills come as naturally as breathing. Not through force or perfect practice, but through patient, consistent engagement with these ideas in your daily life.

This chapter explores how to bridge the gap between knowing and living, between understanding these tools and having them available when you need them most.

MOVING FROM KNOWING TO EMBODYING

When you're learning to drive, every action takes conscious thought. Check mirrors. Signal. Check the blind spot. Turn wheel. Each movement feels mechanical, forced, and unnatural. Your hands grip the steering wheel too tight. Your mind races to remember each step. The simple act of changing lanes becomes a complex sequence demanding all your attention.

But something shifts with practice. Each movement flows more naturally into the next. Your body learns the rhythm of driving. Your hands know how much to turn the wheel. Your feet find the right pressure for brakes and gas. Eventually, you drive home while thinking about dinner plans or listening to music, the mechanics of driving now living in your muscle memory.

Working with emotions follows this same pattern. At first, you consciously remind yourself to breathe during stress, to notice your thoughts without fighting them, and to check in with your body when anxiety rises. Each tool feels separate, requiring effort to remember and use. But gradually, with practice, these responses begin to come naturally. Your body learns new ways to handle old challenges.

Let me show you how this integration happens.

The Learning Cycle

Learning new emotional skills follows a natural progression. It begins with understanding—grasping concepts like how deep breathing calms your nervous system or why mindfulness helps with anxiety. But knowledge alone isn't enough. When you try applying these tools in real moments, you might forget them entirely or find they feel awkward and forced. This gap between knowing and doing is normal, not a sign of failure.

The key is practicing in low-pressure situations, giving your brain chances to build new patterns when stakes feel manageable. Like testing deep breathing when only slightly stressed, not during peak anxiety. Through consistent practice, these skills gradually become automatic—your body remembers what your mind learned. Small successes accumulate into natural responses, transforming intellectual understanding into embodied wisdom.

COMMON INTEGRATION POINTS

Certain moments challenge our skills more than others. That first minute of a difficult conversation, when emotions run high before any words are spoken. The night before a big presentation, when all your calm practice seems to vanish. The instant someone criticizes your work before you can remember your self-compassion tools.

These moments reveal where knowledge hasn't fully integrated into action yet. They show exactly where theory meets reality, where practice meets pressure, and where learned skills face real tests. Instead of seeing these as failures, we can use them as clear signals showing what needs more attention.

Quick Reset Practice

When emotions run high during difficult conversations, before presentations, or after criticism, our practiced skills often seem to vanish. These moments aren't failures but signals showing where we need more integration. Here's a quick reset practice for these challenging times:

60-Second Reset:

1. Notice the need—physical tension, racing thoughts, or emotional intensity.

2. Find a comfortable position, feet grounded.

3. Take three slow breaths, focusing on the exhale
4. On each breath, silently count: "one" (inhale), "and" (exhale)
5. Notice any shift in your body or mind

Why This Works: This brief practice interrupts stress patterns, activates your parasympathetic system, and creates space between trigger and response. So when you're down with the practice, reflect on the changes that you noticed during your mindful breathing.

RESET PRACTICE TRACKER

WEEK OF: _____

MONDAY

Time: _____

Trigger: _____

Body Sensations: _____

Intensity Before (1-10): _____ Intensity After (1-10): _____

What Worked: _____

TUESDAY

Time: _____

Trigger: _____

Body Sensations: _____

Intensity Before (1-10): _____ Intensity After (1-10): _____

What Worked: _____

WEDNESDAY

Time: _____

Trigger: _____

Body Sensations: _____

Intensity Before (1-10): _____ Intensity After (1-10): _____

What Worked: _____

THURSDAY

Time: _____

Trigger: _____

Body Sensations: _____

Intensity Before (1-10): _____ Intensity After (1-10): _____

What Worked: _____

FRIDAY

Time: _____

Trigger: _____

Body Sensations: _____

Intensity Before (1-10): _____ Intensity After (1-10): _____

What Worked: _____

WEEKLY PATTERNS:

Most Common Triggers: ---------------------------------------

Most Helpful Response: ---------------------------------------

What I Learned: ---------------------------------------

Next Week's Focus: ---------------------------------------

Self-Compassion When It's Hard

Self-compassion is letting yourself be uncomfortable, letting yourself work through the hard stuff without letting your heart grow heavy or hard. It means finding ways to face your most difficult emotions, biggest mistakes, and deepest fears without turning against yourself.

Your mind might tell you that being hard on yourself keeps you safe, keeps you improving, and keeps you from making the same mistakes. Like a stern teacher who believes harsh criticism motivates better than encouragement. But this inner harshness often backfires-making you hide from challenges rather than face them, avoid growth rather than embrace it. It carries both softness and strength. It shows up when you acknowledge a mistake without condemning yourself for it. When you feel fear without calling yourself weak for feeling it. When you face difficult emotions without trying to shut them down or push them away.

When you learn something new, you wouldn't expect yourself to master it in a day, or you also wouldn't expect of yourself to learn how to play an instrument in a week. You understand these skills need time, practice, and patience. Your emotional growth deserves this same patient attention, this same understanding of the learning process.

Self-Compassion Practice Sheet

Ever noticed how we remember the exact words of our harshest self-criticism but struggle to recall moments of being kind to ourselves? This happens because we've practiced criticism far more than compassion. Like any skill that goes against habit, self-compassion needs deliberate practice-not in crisis moments, but in quiet spaces where we can lay new foundations.

Set aside 30 minutes when interruptions won't pull at your attention. Find a space that feels private enough for honest reflection. Bring a journal and something to write with. This practice sheet guides you through creating your own personal approach to self-compassion, one that matches how you actually think and feel.

Part 1: Understanding Your Critical Voice

Think of a recent situation where you were hard on yourself. Write down:

❑ What happened?

❑ What did your inner critic say?

❑ How did these thoughts make you feel?

❑ What did you do in response?

Part 2: Finding Your Compassionate

Voice Now approaches the same situation with compassion:

❑ What would you say to a friend in this situation?

❑ What support would help most in this moment?

❑ What's a kinder way to view this situation?

❑ What do you need right now?

Part 3: Creating Your Personal Phrases

Develop phrases that feel authentic to you:

❑ When you make mistakes:

❑ When you feel overwhelmed:

❑ When old patterns resurface:

❑ When you face difficult emotions:

Part 4: Your Daily Practice Plan

Choose specific moments to practice:

❑ Morning routine:

❑ During work/school:

❑ Evening reflection:

❑ Difficult situations:

Return to this worksheet weekly. Notice what works, what needs adjustment, and what supports your growth.

MAKING THESE TOOLS YOUR OWN: A PRACTICE GUIDE

Ever tried to use someone else's glasses? Even if you both need the same general prescription, small differences make their lenses wrong for your eyes. The tools for emotional well-being work similarly-they need precise adjustments to fit your specific needs, your daily rhythms, and your actual life circumstances.

This guide helps you experiment with and adjust these tools until they feel natural to use. Through specific practices and real-life trials, you'll discover exactly how to modify each technique to work for you.

Let me show you how to make these adjustments through practical exercises.

Exercise One: Tool Assessment

Write down every tool you've used in the last month-mindfulness practices, grounding techniques, self-compassion approaches. Note which ones you remember first, and which ones come to mind easily.

For each tool, dig into these questions:

❏ **Success:** When has this tool actually helped? Not in theory, but in real moments. Be specific, that meeting when breathing helped, that morning when grounding worked.

❏ **Barriers:** What stops you from using this tool more often? Look for honest answers; forgetting when stressed, feeling awkward using it, finding it too complex.

❏ **Modifications:** How could you adjust this tool to work better? Maybe shorter versions, different settings, or new approaches that match your style.

Let this assessment guide you toward tools that actually work for your life.

Exercise Two: Daily Integration

Look at your typical day without trying to change it yet. Notice where natural pauses already exist:

❏ That first cup of coffee before everyone wakes

❏ The drive to work or walk to the train

❏ Lunch break at your desk

❑ The shower after work

❑ Those few minutes before sleep

Choose three of these existing pauses. Don't create new ones, use what's already there. These become your practice points.

For each pause, pick one small practice:

❑ **Morning:** Three conscious breaths with your coffee

❑ **Midday:** Quick body scan while waiting for lunch to heat

❑ **Evening:** Brief self-compassion check before bed

Keep each practice short and simple. The goal isn't perfect practice but consistent, small moments of awareness woven through your day.

Exercise Three: Building Your Evidence

Success leaves clues-patterns we can follow to create more successes. For the next two weeks, pay close attention to moments when tools actually help you. Create a simple way to track these moments, whether in your phone notes or a small notebook you carry.

Each time a tool works for you, note:

❑ **The Situation:** What happened? What made you reach for this tool?

❑ What Worked: **Which tool did you use? How exactly did you use it?**

❑ **The Details:** What made it effective in that moment? What specific conditions helped? Body Signals: What changed in your body? What physical signs showed you it worked?

Example: Tuesday morning meeting anxiety Used three breaths while walking to conference room Helped: Walking while breathing felt more natural than sitting still Noticed: Shoulders dropped, mind cleared enough to focus

This log builds concrete evidence of what works specifically for you.

Your practice space matters, and is an important aspect of your practice; let me show you just exactly how to set yours up for success.

Chapter Three

CREATING YOUR HEALING ENVIRONMENT

Homes aren't "found," they're created. Created by carefully choosing what stays and what goes. Created through small touches that make a space feel safe—the soft blanket on your favorite chair, the mug that fits perfectly in your hands, the window that lets in the morning light. Created by learning what helps you feel grounded and what disrupts your peace.

Your healing environment needs this same kind of attention. It grows through understanding what supports you during difficult moments and what makes challenges harder to face. Through knowing when you need quiet and when you need movement, when solitude serves you and when connection helps most.

This chapter explores how to create spaces (both physical and emotional) that support your healing. Not through perfectly arranged rooms or rigid routines, but through mindful choices about what you let into your environment and what you choose to leave out.

Let me show you how to build this kind of healing space.

UNDERSTANDING YOUR SPACE NEEDS

Your environment directly affects how well you practice ACT skills. Notice when and where you concentrate best. Does background noise help you focus, or do you need quiet? Do minimalist spaces clear your mind, or do cozy spaces help you feel secure?

Start tracking the times and places where you naturally feel calmer and more present. You might discover that your kitchen feels peaceful at 6 AM before everyone wakes up, or that your parked car provides a perfect spot for a mindful lunch break. Look for spaces that already help you slow down and check in with yourself.

Creating Your Practice Space

Pick a specific spot that will become your go-to place for ACT work. This creates a mental signal-when you sit here, your brain knows it's time to practice. Your spot needs three key elements:

❑ **Comfort:** Choose a place where you can sit comfortably for 15-20 minutes. Add what you need to feel physically supported-a firm cushion, a backrest, or a soft blanket.

❑ **Minimal Distractions:** Face away from screens and busy areas. Clear the space of items that might pull your attention away. If you share your living space, let others know this is your practice spot and when you need privacy.

❑ **Practical Setup:** Keep your ACT workbook, journal, and pen within arm's reach. Good lighting helps-natural light is great, but a reading lamp works too. Consider keeping a glass of water nearby.

Making Your Space Work

Test different spots until you find what works. Your kitchen table might be perfect in the morning but too busy at dinner time. Your bedroom corner could work well, but you might need to clear some clutter first.

Keep it simple, you really don't need to create a meditation room or buy special equipment. Even a basic chair can become your practice spot if it helps you focus on your ACT work. The key is consistency and practicality.

Quick Tips for Common Situations:

❏ Small living space? Use time instead of place—practice when roommates or family are out.

❏ Open office? Book a meeting room for practice sessions or use your car during breaks.

❏ Busy schedule? Set up two practice spots-one at home and one at work.

❏ Noisy environment? Try noise-canceling headphones or use a white noise app.

Your practice space should make ACT work easier, not become another source of pressure. Start with what you have and adjust as you learn what helps you engage with the work.

Environmental Adjustments

Small changes to your environment can significantly affect your practice quality. Let's look at three key factors you can adjust to support your work.

❏ **Light:** Position near natural light for alertness, adjusting based on the time of day. Keep a lamp handy for cloudy days or evening practice. Find the balance between enough light to stay alert and an atmosphere that supports focus.

❏ **Sound:** Test different sound environments-nature sounds, white noise, or silence. Use headphones in shared spaces or schedule practice during naturally quiet times. Notice which sounds help you maintain focus versus create a distraction.

❏ **Temperature:** Maintain comfortable body temperature to prevent fidgeting and distraction. Keep a blanket nearby for quick adjustments. Ensure good airflow to prevent stuffiness that might affect concentration.

Monitor how these elements interact throughout your day and adjust accordingly. Small environmental changes can significantly enhance your practice quality.

MAPPING YOUR PRACTICE SPACE WORKSHEET

Time & Energy

Best times for practice: _____

Energy level needed: _____

Duration you can maintain focus: _____

Environmental Preferences

Light preference: _____

Natural light: _____

Artificial light: _____

Time of day affects light needs?: _____

Sound preference

Quiet/silence: _____

Background noise: _____

Type of sound that helps focus: _____

Physical Setup

Chosen practice spot: _____

Comfort needs:

❑ Seating: _____

❑ Temperature: _____

❑ Other support needed: _____

Practical Elements

Materials needed close by: _____

Storage solution: _____

How to minimize distractions: _____

Schedule Planning

Morning availability: _____

Midday options: _____

Evening possibilities: _____

Potential Challenges:

Space limitations: _____

Noise issues: _____

Privacy concerns: _____

Solutions I can try: _____

Next Steps:

Three changes I can make today: _____

What I need to gather/buy: _____

When I'll start using this space: _____

Making Practice Work Throughout Your Day

Morning: Choose an easily accessible spot with natural light—a kitchen nook or sunny corner. Keep materials ready for immediate start. Minimal setup removes barriers between waking and practice.

Midday: Identify quick-reset locations for 10-minute breaks. Consider:

❑ Quiet work areas (conference rooms, break rooms)

❑ Outdoor spaces (parks, courtyards)

❑ Your car during lunch breaks

Evening: Create a transition space away from daily activity. Choose a quiet corner with soft lighting that supports reflection. This could be a bedroom chair or living room nook.

Your practice space will evolve. Some days might mean walking practice, others sitting quietly. Focus on finding spaces that support consistent engagement with ACT work, whether at home, work or in between.

Practice Space Evaluation Checklist

Your practice space shapes your ACT work. Use this checklist to assess and refine your chosen areas, ensuring they truly support your practice.

Physical Space:

❑ Comfortable seating

❑ Good lighting

❑ Temperature control

❑ Proper ventilation

❑ Minimal noise disruption

❑ Adequate space for materials

Setup & Access:

❑ Materials within reach

❑ Easy entry/exit

❑ Privacy when needed

❑ Consistent availability

❑ Storage for supplies

❑ Clear of clutter

Focus & Flow:

- ❑ Limited distractions
- ❑ Device-free zone possible
- ❑ Visual calm
- ❑ Sound management
- ❑ Time of day works
- ❑ Others respect the space

What's Working:

Needs Adjustment:

Next Improvements:

EXTRA TIPS FOR PRACTICE SUCCESS

- ❑ Keep a few sensory tools nearby to help ground yourself during difficult moments. A smooth stone to hold, a small essential oil roller, or a textured fidget object can help anchor your attention when anxiety spikes. These tools work especially well during exposure exercises or when working with challenging thoughts.

❏ Create simple visual signals that tell others you're practicing. This might be closing a door halfway or placing a specific item on your desk. If you live or work with supportive people, agree on a gentle signal that means "I need this time." This helps prevent interruptions without making a big announcement every time you practice.

❏ Don't let the weather disrupt your routine. If you usually practice outdoors, have an indoor backup spot ready. If you rely on natural light, check how your space feels on gray days and adjust your lighting. Consider how seasonal changes might affect your practice spots and plan accordingly.

❏ If you use your phone for timing practice sessions or playing ambient sounds, put it in "do not disturb" mode first. Better yet, use a simple timer instead. The fewer tech distractions in your practice space, the easier it is to stay present with the work.

I will always champion the idea that creating the right space for your practice is less about perfection and more about supporting yourself and propelling yourself toward growth and healing. Your practice space, whether a dedicated corner of your home or a quiet spot during lunch break, becomes a physical reminder of your commitment to this work. As you continue with your healing work, let your environment evolve with you. Notice what helps you stay present, what allows you to breathe more easily, and what makes it simpler to show up for yourself day after day. Most importantly, remember that this space—like this practice— is uniquely yours. Trust yourself to create conditions that support your healing, and be willing to adjust as you learn and grow. Your practice space isn't just a physical location; it's a concrete step toward building the life you want to live.

The most effective practice space is the one that helps you do the work consistently. Start where you are, use what you have, and keep what works. Your future self will thank you for creating this foundation for healing and growth.

Now, how you talk to yourself matters, let me show you how the language you use with yourself can be kinder and more compassionate.

Chapter Four

TRANSFORMING SELF-CRITICAL PATTERNS

Shame thrives when we turn our critical voice inward. That constant stream of "not good enough," "should have done better," and "what's wrong with me" creates a trap where anxiety grows and overthinking takes over. Each harsh thought adds weight to the next one until criticism becomes our default response to everything we do.

We often believe this inner harshness helps us improve. We tell ourselves that self-criticism keeps us sharp, motivated, and responsible, but look closer and you'll see how it actually holds us back. Self-criticism drains our energy, increases our anxiety, and makes OCD patterns stronger. It turns simple setbacks into evidence of our supposed failures.

This chapter shows you practical ways to work with self-critical patterns. You'll learn to spot criticism when it shows up, understand what triggers it, and build responses that actually help you move forward. The tools here aren't about positive thinking or forcing yourself to feel better. They focus on creating small shifts in how you talk to yourself, especially during difficult moments.

Think of it like adjusting the volume of your inner dialogue. We're not trying to silence the critical voice completely-we're learning to turn down its intensity so other perspectives can come through. When criticism loosens its grip, you find more room to breathe, think clearly, and choose how to respond.

Let's start by looking at how these critical patterns develop and what keeps them going. This sets the foundation for making real changes in how you relate to yourself.

UNDERSTANDING YOUR INNER CRITIC

Self-criticism always shows up in the most predictable moments; it has a tendency to turn new challenges and small mistakes into evidence of our inadequacy. This harsh inner voice, then speaks in different tones; sometimes attacking directly while other times wrapping criticism in seemingly helpful advice or protective warnings.

These critical thoughts trigger an immediate chain reaction in your body as your chest tightens, breathing becomes shallow, and shoulders creep upward. When your body signals this tension, your brain reads it as confirmation that something's wrong, leading to a cycle where anxiety and protective behaviors grow stronger.

What we need to understand is that these patterns shape our daily choices in subtle but impactful ways. So when we are aware of how our critic operate; its timing, its favorite phrases, its effect on our bodies, we learn how to respond differently. This awareness then becomes the first step toward breaking free from criticism's grip.

Working with Harsh Inner Dialogue

Self-criticism acts as a misguided protector, pointing out every possible flaw before others can. We believe staying alert to our shortcomings shields us from failure or rejection. If we criticize ourselves first, maybe others won't need to. If we spot all our flaws first, maybe we can fix them before anyone notices.

This protective drive backfires. Harsh self-talk amplifies anxiety and strengthens OCD patterns by keeping us hyper-focused on potential problems. When we constantly watch for what might go wrong, our nervous system stays on high alert. Make a small mistake at work, and your critic jumps in with "You always mess things up." This triggers doubt, leading to repeated checking, which only reinforces the belief that constant vigilance keeps you safe.

Breaking this cycle starts with recognizing that your critic isn't protecting you—it's keeping you stuck. Instead of fighting these thoughts, practice noticing them with curiosity. What triggers them? What are they trying to accomplish? This understanding creates space to respond differently when criticism shows up.

How Self-Criticism Affects The Nervous System

A well-regulated nervous system is in a body that is unafraid to feel its feelings, to move through discomfort, and to stay present with challenging experiences. But when self-criticism is our default response, it disrupts this natural regulation and keeps our threat detection system switched on.

Your body reacts instantly when criticism hits. Your muscles tighten, your breathing gets shallow, and your heart speeds up. These physical responses tell your brain "Danger!" even though the threat comes from your own thoughts. Each burst of self-criticism sends stress hormones flooding through your system, making it hard to think clearly or respond flexibly.

Self-criticism tricks your body into treating everyday moments as emergencies. A minor mistake feels like proof you'll always fail. A moment of uncertainty becomes evidence you can't handle life's challenges. Your body reacts to these thoughts as if facing real danger, kicking into fight-flight-freeze when you need to stay calm and think clearly.

This alert state creates a cycle where anxiety and criticism feed each other. Critical thoughts trigger physical tension, which your brain reads as proof that something's wrong. This leads to more criticism, more tension, and a nervous system that can't find its way back to balance.

THE 3-PART RESET WORKSHEET

Let me walk you through a nervous system regulation exercise that helps during moments of harsh self-criticism.

Before The Exercise

Your nervous system needs clear signals to shift out of alert mode. This exercise uses physical movement paired with breathing to send those signals. Think of it as pressing a reset button when criticism winds you up too tight.

First: Get Grounded

Stand up and feel the weight in your feet. Press down through your heels, then your toes. Rock slightly forward and back. This movement reminds your body where it is in space and starts to break the tension pattern that criticism creates.

What I noticed in my feet and legs:

Second: Open Up

Lift your arms slowly to the sides, like wings spreading. As you raise them, breathe in deeply through your nose. Hold this stretched position for a moment. Then let your arms float down as you breathe out through your mouth, making a soft sound. The combination of movement and breath tells your nervous system "I'm safe enough to take up space."

What I felt in my upper body:

Third: Find Your Center

Place one hand on your chest, and the other on your belly. Close your eyes if that feels okay. Take three breaths here, noticing how your body moves with each one. This connects you to your physical self instead of staying stuck in critical thoughts.

Changes I noticed in my breathing:

Overall experience:

Remember: Start with just one round. Notice what changes in your body. You might feel your shoulders drop; your jaw soften, your breathing slow down. These small shifts help break criticism's hold on your nervous system.

Try this when:

❑ You catch yourself in harsh self-talk

❑ Your body feels tight with anxiety

❑ Critical thoughts start looping

❑ You need a quick reset during your day

The power lies in practicing this before criticism hits hard. Run through it a few times when you feel relatively calm. This builds the pathway in your brain, making it easier to use when you really need it. You don't necessarily need to feel totally different after doing this. Even a tiny shift in physical tension will keep you more flexible in your responses to criticism.

Building Healthier Self-Talk

I loved watching my grandmother "be". She would sometimes, while sitting in her garden, close her eyes and whisper words to herself—quiet affirmations that seemed to lift her spirit and ground her in the moment.

When we constantly fill our minds with harsh criticism, we carve deep grooves of negative self-talk. These mental pathways become our default, coloring how we see ourselves and our place in the world. Affirmations work by creating new pathways—not through empty positivity, but through deliberate, grounded statements that align with who we want to be.

Think of affirmations as seeds you plant in your mind. Each time you speak one, you water that seed. The key lies in choosing statements that feel true and possible, even if challenging. "I handle difficult moments with grace" works better than "Nothing bad will ever happen to me." The first statement gives you room to grow; the second denies reality.

Effective affirmations connect to your values and actual experiences. Instead of "I am always happy," try "I can feel my feelings without being overwhelmed by them." Rather than "Everyone loves me," consider "I bring kindness to my interactions with others." These statements acknowledge both challenge and capability.

The power of affirmations shows up most clearly when we pair them with awareness of our current self-talk. Notice when your inner critic speaks up. What does it say? Now imagine how you might respond to a friend saying those same words. This contrast helps you develop affirmations that genuinely support your growth.

Using Affirmations

Anxiety, OCD, and overthinking often fill our minds with doubts, fears, and harsh judgments, but while affirmations can't cure these challenges, they do give us alternative messages that we can work with. especially during difficult moments. These new tools are in your mental toolkit, ready to use when old patterns start to take over.

These affirmations focus on three specific areas. For anxiety, they help ground you in your ability to handle uncertainty and move through fear. For overthinking, they remind you that not every thought needs analysis or action. And for OCD, they support you in trusting yourself and recognizing your strength beyond the disorder.

Choose the affirmations that resonate most with you. Write them down, adjust their wording to fit your voice, and practice them when your symptoms feel less intense. This builds familiarity, making them more accessible when you really need them.

Anxiety Affirmations:

- ❑ "I breathe through discomfort, knowing it will pass."

- ❑ "My anxiety is a part of me, not all of me."

- ❑ "I handle challenges one step at a time."

- ❑ "This feeling is temporary, and I am safe."

- ❑ "I've moved through difficult moments before."

- ❑ "My body knows how to return to calm."

- ❑ "I can feel afraid and still take action."

- ❑ "Each breath steadies me."

- ❑ "I trust my ability to handle what comes."

- ❑ "Fear is a feeling, not a fact."

- ❑ "I am stronger than my anxious thoughts."

- ❑ "My peace matters more than perfection."

- ❑ "I choose which thoughts to act on."

- ❑ "Right now, in this moment, I am okay."

- ❑ "I move at my own pace through challenges."

OCD Affirmations:

- ❑ "I am not my intrusive thoughts."

- ❑ "I can sit with uncertainty."

- ❑ "My worth exists beyond my OCD."

❑ "I trust my first response."

❑ "Discomfort will not break me."

❑ "I release what I cannot control."

❑ "My mind can play tricks, but I stay grounded."

❑ "I choose flexibility over rigidity."

❑ "Time spent on rituals is time I can reclaim."

❑ "I build new patterns with each choice."

❑ "My capacity for healing grows daily."

❑ "I respond rather than react."

❑ "Doubt is normal, acting on doubt is optional."

❑ "I am learning to let go."

❑ "My intuition grows stronger each day."

Overthinking Affirmations:

❑ "Not every thought needs my attention."

❑ "I can observe thoughts without chasing them."

❑ "Simple answers can be true answers."

❑ "My mind is a tool, not my master."

❑ "I choose peace over endless analysis."

❑ "Some questions don't need answers today."

❑ "I trust my initial judgment."

❑ "Clarity comes with calm."

❑ "I can think without spiraling."

❑ "My worth isn't tied to solving everything."

❑ "I release the need to know everything."

❑ "One step at a time is enough."

❑ "I embrace simplicity when possible."

❑ "My thoughts are visitors, not facts."

❑ "I return to the present moment."

Creating Words That Help You Heal: An Exercise

Our minds fill with certain thoughts in moments of challenge and distress. Some thoughts cut deep with criticism, shame, and judgment. Yet, we hold the power to create different messages—ones that speak to both our struggles and our strengths. When anxiety floods in, when OCD patterns tighten their grip, or when overthinking takes over, we need words that ground us in what matters.

The most powerful healing words mix honesty with possibility. They acknowledge our current reality while making space for growth. Through simple, clear statements, we remind ourselves of our capacity to move through difficult moments and work with whatever shows up.

This exercise guides you toward creating messages that resonate with your experience. It helps you find words that feel authentic rather than forced, supportive rather than dismissive. These become anchors you can return to when old patterns arise.

BUILDING YOUR OWN SUPPORTIVE STATEMENTS

Start With What Hurts

Write down three thoughts that repeat in your hardest moments:

Look For What You Need

Under each difficult thought, write what would help in those moments:

Create New Messages

Turn each difficult thought into something that supports you:

From: To:

From: To:

From: To:

From: To:

Make Each Word Count

Adjust until the words feel natural to you:

Try Them Out

Note which statements:

Feel possible: --

Need adjustment: ---

Feel most supportive: -------------------------------------

Remember: Your statements should feel real to you, point toward growth, match your voice, and address your real struggles.

You're in this for a long time and that will require you to be consistent. Let's go have a look at what we can do to ensure that our practice is sustainable for the long haul.

Chapter Five

SUSTAINING LONG-TERM GROWTH

Consistency is hard, especially harder when you're the one who has to keep yourself accountable, but just because it's hard, it doesn't mean it's impossible. Growth happens in small moments, in quiet choices, in the days when you feel like nothing's changing but you show up anyway.

What matters most isn't the big breakthroughs or the perfect practice sessions. It's the ordinary Tuesday when anxiety runs high and you use your tools anyway. It's the moment you catch yourself in an OCD loop and pause, even if you can't fully step out of it yet. It's choosing to work with overthinking rather than fighting it, even when that feels like the harder path.

Long-term change builds through these small moments of showing up for yourself. Some days you'll feel strong, ready to face whatever comes. On other days, you'll barely manage the basics—and that's okay too. Real growth includes all of it: the progress, the setbacks, the clarity, and the confusion.

This chapter looks at how to keep going when motivation fades, when old patterns try to pull you back, or when life gets too busy for perfect practice. You'll learn practical ways to track your progress without getting caught in measurement. Most importantly, you'll discover how to build momentum that carries you through both the easy and hard days.

MAINTAINING PROGRESS

"If you want to go fast, go alone. If you want to go far, go together." This African proverb captures sustainable progress. While anxiety, OCD, and overthinking push us toward quick fixes, lasting change requires understanding how you actually move through your days, not how you think you should.

Sustainable change starts with your natural rhythms. Notice when you focus best, when energy peaks and dips, and how challenges fit into your schedule. Small adjustments often stick better than grand transformations; a new response to stress, or a slight shift in handling anxiety. Link these changes to existing habits: morning coffee becomes a values check-in, and afternoon walks pair with mindful breathing. Success comes from working with your patterns rather than fighting them. Let your progress fit your real life, not an ideal version of how change should look.

ACT MAINTENANCE & GROWTH PLAN

Regular Practice

Daily Skills (choose 2-3)

Weekly Focus

What worked well: _____

Challenges faced: _____

Adjustments needed: _____

Monthly Review

Progress noted: _____

Areas for attention: _____

Plan updates: _____

Growth Goals

3-Month Goals

_____

_____

_____

6-12 Month Goals

Key areas to develop: _____

Skills to strengthen: _____

Support needed: _____

Handling Setbacks

Prevention Strategies

Warning signs to watch: _____

Support system contacts: _____

Daily practices to maintain: _____

Response Plan

First steps when struggling: ------------------------------------

People to contact: ---

Proven strategies: ---

Learning From Setbacks

What triggered this?: --

What helped most?: ---

Changes to make: ---

Review monthly. Remember: Progress isn't perfect-it's about consistent, workable responses to life's challenges.

THE POWER OF ACCOUNTABILITY

Self-accountability sounds A LOT LIKE:

❑ *I'll start Monday*

❑ *This time will be different*

❑ *I really mean it now*

❑ *Just one more day of [insert behavior]*

We had all made promises when we were feeling most motivated, swearing this time things would change. These words feel powerful when we say them, loaded with determination and hope. But they often float away like morning mist, leaving us back where we started.

Real accountability needs more structure than good intentions. It requires more than passionate promises made late at night or desperate deals we make with ourselves during tough moments. True accountability builds on understanding how change actually works in our lives.

Think about how many times you've tried to hold yourself accountable through willpower alone. Through stern self-talk and rigid rules. Through promises written in journals or spoken into mirrors. These methods might work for a day, a week, or even a month. But lasting change demands a different approach.

Let's look at what actually works to keep us on track, starting with understanding different types of accountability and how they support lasting growth.

Different Types of Accountability

Internal Accountability creates a clear structure for your personal growth through specific, measurable actions. You build this foundation by stating exactly what you will do and when you will do it. Writing "I will check my anxiety levels at breakfast and dinner" works better than vague promises about paying attention to anxiety. As you track these commitments through habit charts or journal entries, you learn to trust your own words while discovering patterns in your behavior.

External Accountability strengthens your progress by connecting you with others who support your growth. A therapist offers professional guidance and regular check-ins to help you stay on course. Friends who understand your goals provide encouragement during tough moments without judgment or pressure. Support groups connect you with others facing similar challenges, creating a community where you both give and receive support through shared experiences.

Personal System Accountability turns your environment and daily routines into powerful allies for change. Your space and schedule work together to remind you of your commitments and make healthy choices more natural. Morning alarms signal breathing practice time while written reminders in key spots prompt quick grounding exercises throughout your day. A dedicated evening reflection spot helps you track your progress and plan for tomorrow.

Essentially, each of these work together to support lasting change. Internal accountability builds self-trust, external accountability provides guidance and support, while system accountability makes healthy choices more automatic. When combined thoughtfully, they create a strong framework for maintaining progress even when motivation fluctuates.

Building Check-in Systems

A check-in system creates regular points to assess your progress. These moments task a clear snapshot of where you stand with your anxiety, OCD, or overthinking patterns.

Daily check-ins:

Pick one specific time each day, like with your morning coffee or before bed. Rate your anxiety level from 1-10. Note any OCD patterns that appeared. Write two sentences about what helped or hindered you today. Keep it brief but consistent.

Weekly reviews:

Set aside 15 minutes each Sunday to look at your week. Ask yourself:

❑ What situations triggered anxiety most?

❑ When did I handle challenges well?

❑ What tools did I use successfully?

❑ What patterns do I notice?

Monthly Progress Check

On the first of each month, take a broader view. Read through your daily notes. Look for bigger patterns. Notice which tools you use most often and which ones you avoid. Consider what needs adjusting in your practice.

Focus your tracking:

Choose three specific things to monitor:

❑ Overall anxiety level each day

❑ Times you used a specific tool (like breathing exercises)

❑ Situations that challenged you most

Keep the Format Simple Use a basic 1-10 scale for anxiety levels Write one sentence about what worked Mark an X when you practice your tools Note major triggers with a quick symbol or word

This system grows stronger as you use it. Start with just daily anxiety ratings. Once that feels natural, add one more element. Build slowly so each piece sticks before adding another.

SELF-ACCOUNTABILITY TOOLS

Notebooks and Written Records

A single notebook serves as your main tracking tool. Draw simple charts to mark each time you practice breathing exercises. Write down when anxiety spikes or what triggers OCD patterns. Include notes about what helps and what doesn't. Write the date on each entry so you can track changes over time.

Time Management Tools

Mark your calendar with clear practice times: "7 am-Morning breathing" or "12 pm-Anxiety check-in." These times tell you exactly when to practice your new skills. Use your phone alarm to remind you of these times. Start with one or two set practice times before adding more.

Quick Capture Methods

Keep a notes app open on your phone or a small notepad in your pocket. When you notice something important about your anxiety or OCD patterns, write it down immediately. "Tuesday 10 am-Traffic made anxiety spike" or "2 pm-Used breathing exercise, helped calm down."

Digital Tracking

Simple apps help monitor your daily experiences:

❑ Use a basic mood tracker to rate anxiety levels from 1-10 each day
❑ Set timers for practice sessions like "5 min breathing exercises"
❑ Add reminders to your phone calendar for daily check-ins

Pick tools that:

❑ You already know how to use
❑ Take less than a minute to use each time
❑ Give you clear information about your progress
❑ Feel easy to keep using every day

LONG TERM INTEGRATION

If you're in it for the long haul, then you know change doesn't ask that you follow a perfect script, it just ask of you to take these tools and make them truly yours; to adapt them to fit your life as it shifts and changes.

Moving beyond this workbook means trusting yourself more. The pages here offer structure, but your experience shows you what works. Pay attention when certain tools click instantly while others need adjusting. Notice which practices feel natural and which ones you resist. This information guides how you integrate these skills into your daily life.

Tools change as you do. What helps during high anxiety might shift as you learn to manage your nervous system better. Your OCD responses might need different approaches as you build confidence. Let your practices evolve with you. Adjust breathing techniques to fit new situations. Modify grounding exercises to match your changing needs.

Flexibility matters more than perfection. Some days call for intense practice, others just need basic maintenance. Your tools should bend with life's demands without breaking. When work gets busy, simplify your practice. During calmer periods, explore deeper. This flexibility keeps your skills relevant and useful.

Building resilience happens through this constant adaptation. Each time you adjust a tool to fit a new situation, you get stronger. Every moment you choose to work with anxiety instead of fighting it builds your capacity to handle future challenges. This creates true durability-not because you're doing everything perfectly, but because you're learning to flow with change.

A Letter to Your Future Self

This exercise invites you to celebrate growth-both what you've already achieved and what's still unfolding. Write to yourself six months from now, acknowledging your courage in facing challenges and your commitment to living with greater psychological flexibility.

Writing Prompts:

❏ What small victories are you proud of?

❏ Which ACT skills have helped most?

❏ What would you like your future self to remember?

❏ What growth do you see possible?

Dear Future Me,

Remember when anxiety used to stop you from speaking up in meetings? Today I watched you share an idea even though your voice shook a little. That's growth. You're learning to make space for nervous feelings while moving toward what matters.

I'm proud of how you've started catching those OCD loops earlier, not beating yourself up when they show up but meeting them with more understanding. Those three-breath pauses you've been practicing? They're adding up to real change.

There are still hard days, of course. But you're handling them differently now—less fighting with thoughts, more focus on small steps forward. Keep trusting this process. Keep remembering that courage isn't about feeling fearless but about choosing what matters even when fear shows up.

You're growing in ways that might feel small day by day but add up to real change. Keep going. Keep practicing. Keep showing up for yourself.

With pride in how far we've come,

[Your name]

[Today's date]

YOUR LETTER:

The work you have done and still are going to do matters. Each breath through anxiety, each step back from OCD patterns, each moment you catch overthinking—these add real skills to your life. The tools in this chapter work because they adapt and grow with you. Your accountability system keeps you steady while environmental anchors guide you through tough moments. You learn what helps just by paying attention, by showing up, and by staying curious about your own experience.

This chapter ends, but your relationship with these practices continues. Take them with you. Shape them to fit your life. Trust what you know about what works for you. The strength of these tools lies in how you use them, not in following them perfectly.

Conclusion

You know your body knows; your nervous system knows that healing moves at its own speed. Not through forced change or rigid rules, but through steady practice and a clear understanding of what works. Your hands hold real tools now, ones that make sense in the middle of anxiety, during OCD spikes, through overthinking spirals

The strength you have built comes from doing the work, from trying things out, from learning what actually helps. These skills stick because they fit your life, because you shaped them to match your needs, and because you know how to use them when things get tough. Like a well-worn path, these practices have become familiar ground beneath your feet.

Keep refining what works, notice which practices feel most natural, when certain tools help most, and how to adjust them as you grow. This work matters because it changes how you meet each moment, and how you handle what life brings. No magic solutions, just real skills for real life. So, what will you practice today, as you continue building this path?

References

10 mindfulness exercises to include in your daily routine. (2023, September 1). Calm Blog. https://www.calm.com/blog/mindfulness-exercises

A complete guide to the wheel of life. (2023, September 21). Blossom Themes. https://blossomthemes.com/wheel-of-life/

Ackerman, C. (2017, March 20). *25 CBT techniques and worksheets for cognitive behavioral therapy*. PositivePsychology.com. https://positivepsychology.com/cbt-cognitive-behavioral-therapy-techniques-worksheets/

Asana. (n.d.). *It's time to get your work anxiety under control*. Asana. https://asana.com/resources/work-anxiety

Bailey, R. (2019). Goal setting and action planning for health behavior change. *American Journal of Lifestyle Medicine*, *13*(6), 615–618. https://doi.org/10.1177/1559827617729634

BeaconMM. (2024, January 5). *The power of mindfulness: Techniques and benefits for mental health*. Dana Behavioral Health; Dana Behavioral Health Behavioral Health Services. https://www.danabehavioralhealth.org/the-power-of-mindfulness-techniques-and-benefits-for-mental-health/

Brennan, D. (2021, October 25). *Black and white thinking*. WebMD. https://www.webmd.com/mental-health/black-and-white-thinking

Britt, K. (2011, June 14). *How to change your mind and your life by using affirmations*. Tiny Buddha. https://tinybuddha.com/blog/how-to-change-your-mind-and-your-life-by-using-affirmations/

CBT worksheets. (2012). Therapist Aid. https://www.therapistaid.com/therapy-worksheets/cbt/none

Cisler, J. M., Olatunji, B. O., Feldner, M. T., & Forsyth, J. P. (2009). Emotion regulation and the anxiety disorders: An integrative review. *Journal of Psychopathology and Behavioral Assessment*, *32*(1), 68–82. https://doi.org/10.1007/s10862-009-9161-1

Cognitive Distortions List,. (2024). James Fitzgerald Therapy. https://www.jamesfitzgeraldtherapy.com/cognitive-distortions-list/

Cuncic, A. (2019). *Top tips for managing public speaking anxiety*. Verywell Mind. https://www.verywellmind.com/tips-for-managing-public-speaking-anxiety-3024336

Gaines, J. (2020, November 17). *The philosophy of ikigai: 3 examples about finding purpose*. PositivePsychology.com. https://positivepsychology.com/ikigai/

García-Monge, A., Guijarro-Romero, S., Santamaría-Vázquez, E., Martínez-Álvarez, L., & Bores-Calle, N. (2023). Embodied strategies for public speaking anxiety: Evaluation of the corp-oral program. *Frontiers in Human Neuroscience*, *17*. https://doi.org/10.3389/fnhum.2023.1268798

Journaling tips for beginners to encourage a meaningful Life. (2022, February 2). BALANCE through SIMPLICITY. https://balancethroughsimplicity.com/journaling-tips-for-beginners/

Jouvent, R., Bungener, C., Morand, P., Millet, V., Lancrenon, S., & Ferreri, M. (1999). Distinction between anxiety state/trait in general practice: a descriptive study]. *L'Encephale*, *25*(1), 44–49. https://pubmed.ncbi.nlm.nih.gov/10205733/

Moore, C. (2019, March 4). *Positive daily affirmations: Is there science behind it?* Positive Psychology. https://positivepsychology.com/daily-affirmations/

Perry, E. (2023, March 21). *How to start journaling for mental health: 7 tips and techniques.* BetterUp. https://www.betterup.com/blog/how-to-start-journaling

Ph.D, K. G. (2023, June 20). *How to overcome social anxiety: 8 techniques & exercises.* Positive Psychology. https://positivepsychology.com/social-anxiety/

Phil Gowler. (2018, March 20). *The parent-adult-child model. simple yet it works!* Phil Gowler. https://www.philgowler.co.uk/therapies/the-parent-adult-child-model-simple-yet-it-works/

Positive affirmations for anxiety: Reframing your worry to calm down. (2022, April 25). Psych Central. https://psychcentral.com/anxiety/affirmations-for-anxiety

Powers, T. (2024, June 11). *Strategies for thriving in the face of challenges in the fast-paced and unpredictable world of today's work environment, well-being and resilience have become essential components of personal and professional success. as individuals and organizations navigate through ongoing challenges and uncertain.* Linkedin.com. https://www.linkedin.com/pulse/nurturing-well-being-work-tara-powers-tgxxc

SAMHSA. (2019). Setting goals and developing specific, measurable, achievable, relevant, and time-bound objectives. In *SAMHSA*. https://www.samhsa.gov/sites/default/files/nc-smart-goals-fact-sheet.pdf

Scherer, H. (2018, October 12). *The wheel of life – your first step to living life on purpose.* Holly Scherer. https://www.hollyscherer.com/wheel-of-life/

Science of the mindset. (2024, April 24). Science of the Mindset. https://www.scienceofthemindset.com/blog/finding-your-own-50-shades-of-grey-breaking-free-from-cognitive-distortions-and-overcoming-black-and-white-thinking

Stanborough, R. J. (2022, October 25). *Cognitive distortions: 10 examples of distorted thinking.* Healthline. https://www.healthline.com/health/cognitive-distortions

Stein, D. J., Craske, M. G., Rothbaum, B. O., Chamberlain, S. R., Fineberg, N. A., Choi, K. W., Jonge, P., Baldwin, D. S., & Maj, M. (2021). The clinical characterization of the adult patient with an anxiety or related disorder aimed at personalization of management. *World Psychiatry, 20*(3), 336–356. https://doi.org/10.1002/wps.20919

Stibich, M. (2020, December 15). *How to make your health goals S.M.A.R.T.* Verywell Mind. https://www.verywellmind.com/smart-goals-for-lifestyle-change-2224097

The difference between trait and state anxiety: Part I. (2022, February 11). Khiron Clinics. https://khironclinics.com/blog/the-difference-between-trait-and-state-anxiety-part-i/

Transactional analysis. (n.d.). Www.businessballs.com. https://www.businessballs.com/emotional-intelligence/transactional-analysis-eric-berne/

What is black and white thinking and 9 ways to stop it in it's tracks - that's so well. (2023, August). That's so Well - Therapy for Women. https://thatssowell.com/what-is-black-and-white-thinking-and-9-ways-to-stop-it-in-its-tracks/

Wheel of life: How it helps you find balance. (n.d.). Better Up. https://www.betterup.com/blog/wheel-of-life

Made in the USA
Monee, IL
10 May 2025

17202668R00167